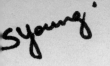

RUTH S. KEMPE is Associate Professor of Paediatrics and Psychiatry at the University of Colorado; C. Henry Kempe is Professor of Paediatrics and Microbiology at the same institution. Henry Kempe is widely regarded as the leading authority on child abuse, and first described 'the battered baby syndrome'.

The Editors of THE DEVELOPING CHILD

JEROME BRUNER helped found the Center for Cognitive Studies at Harvard in 1960, and served there as Director until 1972. He is currently Watts Professor of Psychology at the University of Oxford and Fellow of Wolfson College, Oxford. He has long been interested in the nature of perception, thought, learning, and language, and has published widely on these topics. At present he is focusing his research on the early development of language in infants and on the role of the pre-school in early child development.

MICHAEL COLE is Director of the Laboratory of Comparative Human Cognition, at the Rockefeller University in New York. Trained initially as a psychologist, his research in recent years has led him into the fields of anthropology and linguistics in an attempt to understand better the influence of different cultural institutions, especially formal schooling, on the development of children. He is editor of *Soviet Psychology*, and his most recent book, co-authored with Sylvia Scribner, is entitled *Culture and Thought*.

BARBARA LLOYD is Reader in Social Psychology at the University of Sussex, author of *Perception and Cognition: a Cross-Cultural Perspective*, and editor (with John Archer) of *Exploring Sex Differences*. Her interest in child development has always been strongly cross-cultural (her first research was published as part of the Whiting's *Six Cultures* study). She has recently investigated cognitive development among both English and Nigerian children.

# THE DEVELOPING CHILD *edited by*
Jerome Bruner   Michael Cole   Barbara Lloyd

# CHILD ABUSE

Ruth S. Kempe and C. Henry Kempe

FONTANA/OPEN BOOKS

First published in 1978 by Fontana/Open Books
and Open Books Publishing Ltd
Copyright © Ruth S. Kempe and C. Henry Kempe, 1978

A hardback edition of *Child Abuse* is available from
Open Books Publishing Ltd, 11 Goodwin's Court,
London WC2N 4LB

To Brandt Steele, beloved friend and colleague
with our thanks

# Contents

# Editors' Preface

Recent decades have witnessed unprecedented advances in research on human development. Each book in *The Developing Child* reflects the importance of this rese rch as a resource for enhancing children's well-being. It is the purpose of the series to make this resource available to that increasingly large number of people who are responsible for raising a new generation. We hope that these books will provide rich and useful information for parents, educators, child-care professionals, students of developmental psychology and all others concerned with childhood.

JEROME BRUNER, *University of Oxford*
MICHAEL COLE, *The Rockefeller University*
BARBARA LLOYD, *University of Sussex*

# Acknowledgements

The authors express their gratitude for the encouragement and support received from the Robert Wood Johnson Foundation and the William R. Grant Foundation. This book was written at the Rockefeller Study Center at Bellagio whose hospitality we valued.

# Part I

# The Nature of
# Child Abuse

# 1/The Dimensions of the Problem

A book on child abuse could not have been written one hundred years ago. If an investigator from the 1970s were to be transported back to the nineteenth century so that he could survey the family scene with modern eyes, child abuse would be clearly visible to him. In the past, however, it was largely invisible to families and their communities. Before it could be acknowledged as a social ill, changes had to occur in the sensibilities and outlook of our culture.

Historically society has not been troubled by the maltreatment of children. Where children were not wanted, mortality ran high. In nineteenth-century London, for example, 80 per cent of the illegitimate children who were put out to nurse died; unscrupulous nurses collected their fees and then promptly did away with the babies. When a profit could be made, adults sometimes sold children into slavery or used them as a source of cheap labour. This is not to say that the individual parents did not care about their children; but pervasive values sanctioned many practices that we now call abusive, and even caring parents were under their influence. Infanticide was not only a threat to the infants of royal families; in some cultures it had wide acceptance as a means of controlling population size and eliminating children with birth defects. Mutilation of children is usually presumed to be a remote custom. Examples such as the foot binding of Chinese girls and the cranial deformations of certain Indian groups come readily to mind. Yet mutilation of the sexual organs has been seen as a religious rite since the Stone Age, and in spite of its questionable value, circumcision is still the most common operation performed in Western medicine today.

In order to chart the gradually emerging awareness of child abuse – as of any other social issue, such as women's suffrage or the civil rights of minorities – it is necessary to point to a moment in time when it is clear that established values began to weaken their hold. Certainly a carelessness (and ignorance) about the physical and emotional needs of developing children was the norm for a long time, but maltreatment of children has survived into the late twentieth century, virtually unchallenged, because two beliefs remained strong. First, children were seen as their parents' property and it was taken for granted that parents had every right to treat their children as they saw fit; furthermore they were seen as their parents' responsibility, and for many centuries harsh treatment was justified by the belief that severe physical punishment was necessary to maintain discipline, transmit educational decisions, and expel evil spirits. In the schools of Sumer 5000 years ago there was a 'man in charge of the whip' to punish boys upon the slightest pretext. The ancient philosophers beat their pupils unmercifully. Later, there was a time in most christian countries when children were whipped on Innocents' Day to make them remember the massacre of the innocents under Herod. Parents, teachers, and ministers alike have believed that the only cure for the 'foolishness bound up in the heart of a child' was repression by the rod, and 'beating the devil out of him'* is still a common expression today.

There were, it is true, occasional periods of protest and history reveals influential individuals who spoke out against the maltreatment of children. Plato, in 400 B.C., advised teachers to 'train children not by compulsion but as if they were playing', and Sir Thomas More used peacock feathers to beat his daughters. But respites were short-lived for the

---

* We have generally used the male pronoun when referring to a child, only because it is then easier to distinguish him (or her) from mothers and other female caregivers.

ighly vulnerable children, and firmly held values decreed that what happened to them was a family affair.

The change in cultural views can be traced to the early days of the Child Welfare Movement in America. In New York in 1825 the New York Society for the Reformation of Juvenile Delinquents established a house of refuge, primarily for wayward children and only secondarily for the neglected and abused. The Society for the Prevention of Cruelty to Children was founded in New York City in 1871, and, following its example, many other societies with similar objectives were formed in different parts of the United States and Great Britain, stirring the public conscience on behalf of destitute children. In 1909 the first White House Conference was convened, and the American Association for Study and Prevention of Infant Mortality was founded. Soon it became evident that the causes of child abuse evolved from complex psychosocial backgrounds; little was known, however, about the real nature of the problem and it was rarely diagnosed.

The battered-child sydrome[1] was first described in 1868 by Ambroise Tardieu, a professor of legal medicine in Paris. He had, of necessity, to rely on autopsy findings.[2] He described 32 children battered or burnt to death. The same year Athol Johnson at the Hospital for Sick Children in London called attention to the frequency of repeated fractures in children.[3] He attributed these to the condition of the bones, since rickets at that time was almost universal among London children. We now know that almost every case he described was, in fact, an abused child. Official London records reveal that of the 3926 children under five years of age who died by accident or violence in 1870, 202 deaths were attributed to manslaughter; 95 to neglect; 18 to exposure to cold – all effectively due to child abuse. However, the rickets theory persisted well into the twentieth century.

It was not until 1946 that John Caffey reported his original observations regarding the unexplained association of subdural haematoma and abnormal X-ray changes in long bones.[4] Soon Caffey and Silverman clearly defined their traumatic nature.[5] In 1955 P. V. Woolley and W. A. Evans published a paper in the *Journal of the American Medical Association* entitled 'Significance of Skeletal Lesions in Infants Resembling Those of Traumatic Origin'.[6]

In 1961 Henry Kempe arranged for an interdisciplinary presentation at the Annual Meeting of the American Academy of Pediatrics on the subject of the battered-child syndrome. Our comprehensive description of the syndrome was published the following year in the *Journal of the American Medical Association* and presented paediatric, psychiatric, radiological and legal concepts, as well as providing the earliest incidence figures for the United States.[7] Since 1962 literally thousands of articles and dozens of books have greatly added to the understanding of child abuse and neglect.

Still, the old values have not been demolished: as recently as 1975 the United States Supreme Court ruled that states were permitted to decide if teachers could physically punish children in school. But values are clearly changing; the same act that might have met with applause from clergymen a hundred years ago must be referred to the authorities of criminal justice today. The history of the emergence of child abuse as a social issue involves a growing recognition of maltreatment as an unnecessary evil, the technical capability to trace clues that tell a story of inflicted injury, and the community's readiness to address the problem constructively.

## WHAT IS CHILD ABUSE?

Child abuse involves a hurt child, but the web of cause and effect is imperfectly understood. One approach is to look at the symptoms that the child presents. Another is to look at the actions of the caretaking adults (parents, guardians and friends). Four categories are commonly used to classify their behaviour: physical violence, physical and emotional neglect, emotional abuse, and sexual exploitation. Physical violence implies physically harmful action directed against the child;

it is usually defined by any inflicted injury such as bruises, burns, head injuries, fractures, abdominal injuries, or poisoning. Inflicted injury requires medical attention (whether the child receives it or not).

The borderline between wilful injury and physical neglect, both of which can cause accidental harm, is sometimes difficult to determine, but examples such as giving large adult doses of sedatives to an infant or hallucinogenic drugs to a small child are clearly so dangerous as to constitute abuse.

Neglect can be a very insidious form of maltreatment and, if there is no contact with a doctor or nurse, it can persist, unnoticed, for a long time. Neglect implies the failure of the parent to act properly in safeguarding the health, safety and well-being of the child. Physical neglect includes nutritional neglect, failure to provide medical care, or failure to protect a child from physical and social danger.

Nutritional neglect results from feeding an infant inadequate calories – either simply not enough food or a bizarre diet. It leads to failure to thrive, a potentially life-threatening condition in which the child's weight, height, and often head circumference fall below the third percentile of children his age. Although there are diseases that also cause failure to thrive, more than half of the cases seen are due to inadequate nutrition. The baby is small, gaunt, with prominent bones and no fat padding his cheeks or buttocks; he has an anxious expression and a voracious appetite. Children who suffer from failure to thrive often show other signs of neglect, such as poor hygiene and emotional upset; they relate poorly to others, are depressed, apathetic, and developmentally delayed. Emotional neglect almost always occurs with physical abuse; it can also occur with good physical care and inflict just as much damage on the developing personality. Flagrant cases describe children left locked in an attic; far more common are the subtle forms of emotional abuse in which a child is continually terrorized, berated, or rejected.

Sexual abuse means the exploitation of immature children through such actions as incest, molestation and rape. Its particular circumstances, in both detection and treatment, warrant a discussion of sexual exploitation as a special case (Chapter 4).

Behaviour of the adult – angry, indifferent, seductive – can vary tremendously. Attaching blame to these parents may be difficult to resist. But it is more useful to view their behaviour as an extreme response to stress, and often these parents themselves are suffering individuals who endured abused childhoods. One of the major misconceptions about abusive parents is that they are invariably disadvantaged. Poor parents may well be under more external stress from worries about homelessness, overcrowding or debt than those who are better off, but the crucial internal stresses are remarkably similar for rich and poor parents alike. Another misconception is that abusive parents are fundamentally and incurably abnormal, psychotic, criminal, or retarded. Like the first, this misconception is probably popular because it tends to put a distance between us and them.

A third misconception about child abuse is that it is very rare. In fact, child abuse is reported 320 times per million population in the United States. Reported sexual abuse stands at 150 per million. Since the dimensions of the problem elude precise definition, it is not surprising that disagreements arise concerning the incidence of abuse. Our evidence shows that reported cases represent only a fraction of the total (sexual abuse, especially, is under-reported). Investigators who base their conclusions only on reported cases inevitably underestimate the problem. David Gil, for instance, states that 'the physical consequences of child abuse do not seem to be very serious in the aggregate'.[8] It must be stressed, however, that all of Gil's data from 1965 to 1969 were taken from reported cases only and were collected in the earliest years of the laws regarding reports of abuse.

As public attitudes become more broadly understanding, many more parents voluntarily seek help before they seriously harm their children. In 1968, California had 4000 reported cases; in 1972, 40,000; Florida's reports jumped from 10 cases to 30,000 over the same four years, and Michigan went from 721 to 30,000. Not only are more cases being reported –

they are of a milder nature, suggesting that families are being helped sooner. In Denver, the number of hospitalized abused children who die from their injuries has dropped from 20 a year (between 1960 and 1975) to less than one a year.

Child abuse is a problem – but not a hopeless one. Our results show that four out of five abusive parents can be brought to stop injuring their children physically. This book is for all those people who, in the course of their professional of private lives, may be called on to recognize and cope with cases of child abuse. We hope to provide a clear picture of the nature of abuse and the conditions that give rise to it. There are ways of dealing with the problem which we believe can provide effective treatment in most cases and prevent others from occurring. Our conclusions are based, in large part, on the work of the National Center for the Prevention and Treatment of Child Abuse and Neglect at the University of Colorado School of Medicine, Denver. Those of us who work at the Center can now look back on twenty years of experience with over three thousand families in which a child was battered, sexually exploited, seriously neglected, or failed to thrive. These families and their children have taught us a great deal about how to predict abusive and neglectful behaviour and how to recognize it early and treat it promptly. What we have learned has been enough to change dramatically our practices in obstetrics and paediatrics, our use of services such as health visiting, social work, psychology and psychiatry, and our work with the police and the courts.

In this book we will explore the network of cause and effect that entangles abusive parents and their children and the ways in which abuse and neglect can be prevented, treated, and cured.

# 2/The Abusive Parent

There have always been parents who have physically abused their children, but it is only recently that the pervasiveness of the problem has been acknowledged. Only thirty years ago the occasional child brought to the hospital was seen as the odd, dramatic case – unmistakably the victim of a murderous attack. The violence was usually attributed to a drunken father or an inadequate mother, labels that provided little insight. The families involved always seemed to be from the lower socioeconomic classes. But our work during the past twenty years has taught us that abusive parents come from all walks of life, rich and poor, well educated and uneducated, from all races and religious backgrounds. It is possible to describe many characteristics they have in common, but there is no stereotype; the parents do not fit a single psychological pattern that can be given a psychiatric diagnosis.

Rather than look first at extreme cases, it may be helpful to consider neglect and abuse within the whole range of parenting. If we were to draw a graph of all parents, ranged according to their ability, we would probably end up with a familiar bell-shaped curve. At one end would be a single dot, representing the only possible claimant to perfection as a mother, the Madonna, but let us not forget that Mary also had the perfect child. Most of us would fit into the large rounded part of the curve representing those who offer their children excellent, good, or good-enough parenting. At the other end of the spectrum, the curve would not descend steeply; rather it would slope very gradually and might cover some 20 to 30 per cent of parents, all of whom have some difficulty in caring for their children adequately. This is the percentage revealed by our own formal studies, and it agrees with some informal surveys made in hospital clinics and by private paediatricians.

But this figure covers those with *potential* difficulty in parenting, and by no means will all of them be overtly neglectful or abusive. On the contrary, most of them will be parents who are unduly anxious about their abilities, who are poorly informed, or whose abilities to manage their children vary a great deal, with some lapses into difficult periods followed by recoveries to their usual more comfortable style. What makes for the variations? Circumstances, past and present, will support or strain the relationship between parent and child. We shall draw our portrait chiefly by describing these historical and immediate factors and showing how they affect the personality of the abusive parent.

First, we must say a word about parenting. We consider it the ability to recognize (with or without clear understanding) the needs of a child for, first, physical care and protection; second, nurturance; third, love and the opportunity to relate to others; fourth, bodily growth and the exercise of physical and mental functions; and last, help in relating to the environment by way of organizing and mastering experience. In addition to recognizing these needs, a parent must be able to meet them or at least facilitate their being met. Most of this is done without much, or any, conscious thought, certainly without formal knowledge. Perhaps this is where the importance of empathy lies – that automatic understanding of and participation in the child's experience which brings with it the knowledge of what he needs.

There is another important dimension to parenting: the parent has a reward for being a parent, the *knowledge* that the child's needs are being met. This satisfaction is crucial, for at times the child's and the parent's needs will not coincide and may even conflict. It is up to parents to find a way of meeting their own needs that will not interfere with those of their child. A simple example of failure to do this, which happens to have nothing to do with physical abuse, is the behaviour of a parent who wishes to experience through his child successes he himself never had. The father who never excelled at baseball or football gives himself a second chance by pressuring his son to go all out for those games. If that suits the son, they can both share a satisfying hobby. But if the son hates sport, his father may push him into humiliating defeat and then blame him for the disappointment he himself feels.

## CYCLE OF ABUSE

The most consistent feature of the histories of abusive families is the repetition, from one generation to the next, of a pattern of abuse, neglect and parental loss or deprivation. In each generation we find, in one form or another, a distortion of the relationship between parents and children that deprives the children of the consistent nurturing of body and mind that would enable them to develop fully. The parenting may be inadequate because of physical or emotional absence, which early in life results in the failure-to-thrive syndrome. When the parent is consistently absent in the emotional sense, the child can suffer from a deprivation that may go unrecognized. It is found in all social classes and can be seen in those children of the well-to-do who spend their lives with a succession of indifferent nursemaids and in a series of boarding schools and camps.

Emotional abuse, in the absence of physical damage, is difficult to document, but its effects can be crippling; they tend to be diagnosed by psychiatrists and psychologists only years after the event, as the symptoms of emotional disturbance become more obvious. *A priori* we assume that physical abuse and neglect imply the presence of at least some emotional abuse, but the opposite may not always be true. Sometimes the abuse is primarily verbal, and the child is continually told that he is hated, ugly, unlovable, stupid, or an unwanted burden. He may not even be spoken to by name, but called 'You' or 'Freak' or 'Hey, Stupid'. Such a child may find himself made into the family scapegoat, and it may be that his brothers and sisters are actively encouraged and perhaps even rewarded for abusing or ignoring him. The opportunities for emotional abuse are, of course, innumerable and, because the scars are not physical ones, they may go unnoticed. Emotional abuse plays some role in all abuse and neglect; its presence in almost every case we discuss will be amply evident.

No one knows quite how the ability to be a parent is passed on from one generation to the next. Probably the most significant channel is the experience of having been sympathetically parented, of having experienced what it feels like to be an infant, helpless but cherished and nurtured into childhood. This knowledge is not readily accessible because it is acquired before formal thought, memory and speech are operating. Although it is not conclusive proof, some fairly convincing evidence exists that young children do repeat behaviour or experiences from their first two years, which indicates that they were aware, on a non-verbal level, of what was occurring. It is precisely these early traces of pre-verbal experience, which are so difficult to recapture consciously, that may be tormenting the subconscious of the abusive parent and making it so difficult for him to change. Although the memory of mistreatment as a young child is not recoverable as something that the conscious mind can evaluate, the feelings remain, vaguely attached to the concept of a relation between parent and child. If they cannot be recognized, they cannot be understood or justified by the abusive parent, who must come to terms with them in order to alter his behaviour. Undoubtedly most persons who were abused as babies were also abused as they grew into childhood, and these later experiences are certainly remembered. The subsequent experience would reinforce the original traumatic events, but it seems to us that the tenacity with which parents cling to their parenting behaviour owes its strength to the threats to survival they themselves experienced in the time beyond memory. The fear derived from these threats lives on in abusive mothers and fathers; that is why, in relating to them, we must be so ready to cope with their rather primitive and seemingly irrational reactions to comparatively simple situations. Their quick and intense responses to any kind of rejection, real or imagined, illustrate this underlying fear.

The mechanisms by which abusive parents repeat the parenting patterns to which they were exposed are common to us all; it is only the nature of the patterns which differs. We all carry on our heritage, though most of us are unaware of it. There is no question that we are exposed to many constant models of parenting as we observe the treatment of young children in our own families and in the families around us. But our ability to choose among models may well be limited by the nature of our own experience. In a time of crisis for the parent, when the relationship with a child has reached the point of unbearable stress, it is seldom logical thought that governs the parent's behaviour; it is the underlying *tone* of the relationship. That is probably why so many conscientious and interested parents, who have emphatically rejected their own parents' child-rearing methods, may revert in moments of crisis, when their own carefully thought-out methods are not working well, to the methods they have rejected. Then they may find that they have slipped into the patterns they experienced as children. Only if they are aware of what has happened are they able to bring some reasoning to bear on the situation.

## PARENTS' PERCEPTIONS OF CHILDREN

We can start to recognize the nature of a parent-child relationship when we look at how parents perceive their children, their concept of how a child should behave, and what his needs are at a particular age. When a mother sees her child unrealistically, for instance when she thinks her six-month-old is *wilfully* having a bowel movement at an inconvenient time, we know that there is something wrong with her perception of her child. When she is unwilling to revise it and sees physical punishment as the way to teach him how to do right, we know she is potentially abusive. And when she insists that he is trying to make her life difficult, that he is a stubborn child who will grow up delinquent or a burden to her unless she takes steps now, we know that she needs help in understanding why her own needs for feeling secure as a mother should be so threatened by an ill-timed soiled napkin. Abusive parents also see physical punishment as an appropriate way to deal with their babies. They may be discouraged when spanking obviously brings no result, but they truly see no alternative and grow depressed both by their own behaviour and their babies' responses. Helplessly, they continue in the same vicious circle: punishment, deteriorating relationship, frustration, and further punishment.

In addition to the specific effects of abuse or neglect, there is much else than can leave the developing child ill-equipped to form his own life, and ultimately to reach mature adulthood and parenthood. Exactly like their children, abusive parents were, we believe, brought up with images of themselves as bad, worthless, and unlovable. They were brought up to distrust an uncertain, unforgiving world where joy, approval and affection either did not exist or inevitably deteriorated into anger and punishment. They did not learn at home how to please others without depriving themselves of pleasure, or learn that 'give and take' means there is enough for both sides. They probably did not learn many ways of using their intelligence in intellectual tasks, so that school may have found them already disqualified from academic success. If they were particularly withdrawn, anxious, or aggressive, they may have found themselves labelled 'problem children' from the start and may never have even begun to take advantage of school. They may have had trouble making friends, been afraid to trust them, sensitive to rejection, easily given to withdrawing or fighting. Many an abused or deprived child has grown up lonely, unable to make any use of the opportunities offered when he finally leaves the hostile environment of his home, unable to make friends, unable to revise his opinion of himself.

When such children reach adolescence, their need for love becomes more acute. It is then (and often much too early) that the abused or deprived teenager finds a kindred spirit – someone who responds to the need for acceptance with a similar need. Searching for love at any price, these young people do not look too carefully at what is expected in return. Only when marriage and pregnancy have become facts does each partner realize that the burden of providing support and unstinting love for the child is supposed to be jointly theirs – not wholly the other's. Marriage turns out to be another dead end, and the new parents' need for love and acceptance grows more acute than ever. Two badly deprived youngsters struggle together much like two drowning nonswimmers. Having been expected by their own parents to provide the love and total obedience that might engender feelings of success and self-approval, what is more natural than to look for the same thing in their own baby? That this is completely inappropriate is not obvious to young parents now subjected to the same kind of role reversal. 'That's the way it's supposed to be,' they believe.

Whether a mother feels it is right to hit out in frustration and disappointment at her baby, or feels unmoved by his cries of hunger, may depend on how she herself was raised. It also depends on how well she is able to cope with the needs of the baby. Some mothers keep the baby out of consciousness and neglect him severely; others do not neglect his physical needs, but can misperceive their significance and distort his normal behaviour into wrongdoing. Either course can be dangerous or even fatal to the child. The relationship between neglect and abuse is not well understood; they seem to exist together, in differing proportions. But one striking sequence has occurred often enough to note: a mother who has been so neglectful that her baby has suffered from failure to thrive may be recognized and offered treatment. If this treatment does not adequately take into consideration her own need for nurturance, but concentrates only on her responsibilities as a mother, she may become even more abusive towards the child. It is as if she turns her resentment of the authorities' criticism of her behaviour against the baby instead of against the social worker. She blames him for the trouble she is in and, ignoring his troubles, begins to punish him. This fits our finding that mothers of infants admitted to hospital for failure to thrive quite often show in their history and behaviour a high potential for physical abuse. It seems also consistent with the acute need most abusive parents have for nurturance themselves, and with the fact that treatment is usually successful only when those parental needs are met.

## IMPACT OF THE NEW BABY

In addition to their parents' own childhood experiences, there are factors relating to the coming of each specific child, from his conception to the reality of his physical and mental make-up, that make him more or less satisfying to the parents, and therefore more or less likely to be abused. These factors concern not only the additional stress that having a child adds to the parents' lives but the emotional significance the baby has for them as well. From the very beginning of pregnancy, there are factors which may begin to influence unfavourably the outcome for that particular child, and if these considerations, each seemingly trivial in itself, accumulate, the result may be tragedy.

For the mother, an unwanted pregnancy may be complicated by personal problems, including the father's desertion, her own ill health, or a total absence of support from anyone close. It may terminate in premature delivery, a difficult ordeal she must face alone. The prematurity of her baby may cause disappointment, separation, and fear of creating a bond with someone who may not survive – all added to the expense and worry of caring for a child who seems fragile and remote. Lest this seem like melodrama, it is important to emphasize that such situations occur frequently and are normally dismissed as the expected lot of the disadvantaged, unwed, or separated young mother.

Prematurity or the post-natal illness of mother or child adds disproportionately to the burdens of parenting and may exhaust the resources of a potentially abusive parent. An early difficulty (such as a severe feeding problem) may make care sufficiently burdensome to tip the balance. A mature and well-adjusted mother would find such a situation stressful, and to weather the storm she would need to draw on her own inner reserves of strength, as well as the help of those close to her; but the mother who is alone and who has no inner reserves finds herself overwhelmed.

It is the interplay between the inner strength the parents possess or lack, and the stresses of the relation with the new child that determines how catastrophic the outcome will be. Since a potentially abusive mother's inner resources for parenting are so meagre, his circumstances must be just right to allow her to find in her child the satisfaction she seeks. Sometimes this does happen; her marriage, her home and life, and her relations with other people may be rewarding enough to keep her comparatively satisfied and free of stress. If her baby is healthy, attractive, of the sex she prefers, and, above all, easy to feed and manage, she may find herself happy with motherhood and communicate fairly well with her child. The child who can meet his parents' expectations in this way is fortunate. If the 'fit' continues to be good – if he continues to adjust to the kind of care his mother wishes to provide and does not cry or demand anything more – parenthood may seem to be successful. This state, however, is often interrupted when the pressure of the child's developmental needs for increased attention and social interaction, for exploration and autonomy, begin to conflict with the mother's expectation that he is there to give her pleasure and not to make excessive demands on her time and energy. At this point, he must be able to modify his needs and stifle his developmental urges, or his mother will perceive him as naughty and wrong and begin to punish him to be sure he doesn't end up 'spoiled'.

Sometimes parents will have very high expectations of their children before development has progressed very far, expectations almost certain to be thwarted. Only if the child is able to extend himself beyond his natural inclinations and, through inhibition or extra striving, perform as his parents wish, will he avoid their disapproval and punishment; and it will almost certainly be at the cost of spontaneity and social development.

Kay Tennes has described one family:

Keith was seven months old and beginning to have activity which was increasingly irritating to his mother. Activity during nappy changing she found most unbearable and she said, 'I had to whack him again and again to make him hold still.' Keith was observed while being changed, lying completely immobile, intently watching his mother's hands with a serious expression on his face. Three months later, the mother complained that Keith had learned his lesson only too well. During changing and dressing he now became quite limp, failing to hold up his hands to have his shirt put on. Mother said she would 'have to show him he could only go so far before he got the flat of her hand again.'[1]

Parents like this interpret 'cannot' as 'will not'. One little boy of eight months who cried for attention from his playpen was thought to be having a temper tantrum and was beaten so that he wouldn't be spoiled. The same little boy at fourteen months was not allowed to ask for his own toy on the shelf; he could only look and 'politely' wait until offered it by his father. As a young boy this father had been taken to business parties and shown off because of his 'good manners'.

But what about a mother who is so seriously depressed or preoccupied with her own anxieties and needs that she hardly thinks of her baby? She feeds, changes and holds him only according to her own impulses, not when his schedule or even his crying would suggest it. How different is her world from that of luckier, more relaxed mothers, who manage that lively, happy, smiling social interchange in which mother

and baby reciprocally stimulate and respond to each other.
The infant is vivacious, smiling and cooing, straining his
body towards the mother, who gleefully responds to his total
absorption in the excitement of interacting with her. The
very rhythm of this interaction attests to their finely tuned
adjustment. Now that we recognize the baby's innate potential for communicating his own developmental needs, we
understand how important it is that the mother be sensitive to
her child's individuality and able to enmesh her responsiveness and demands with his. We also know that a baby is, as it
were, pre-programmed to respond to his mother or other
primary caregiver in a way that is satisfying to them both.

For the abusive or neglectful mother, such responsiveness
is not possible. Her experience has taught her that babies
have no needs beyond the minimum essential for survival.
Anything beyond that is spoiling and will result in a wilful,
whining child who will grow up to defy her and be nothing
but trouble. When her baby cries because he is hungry or
needs comforting, she misinterprets it as the beginning of the
bad behaviour she dreads. Oblivious to the emaciated state
he reaches, she sees not a starving, helpless infant but some
monstrously greedy parasite who will exhaust her reserves of
food, energy and love. That distortion of reality is not
mediated by adult reasoning, although the mother may seem
intellectually intact and well able to react appropriately in
almost every other way. She probably projects onto her baby
the accumulated unfulfilled wishes of a lifetime – a greed for
love and care so great that it is frightening and cannot be
tolerated lest she be totally engulfed. One can observe how
insatiable such mothers may themselves be for attention and
evidence of caring. Only when some of their own needs have
been met can they discuss and perhaps begin to understand
a child's separate needs.

## CRISES: EXTERNAL AND INTERNAL

It is easy to see why many abusive parents have developed only a limited ability to cope with adult life, and often appear to be immature people, barely able to survive from one crisis to the next. Difficulties in learning, lack of interest in school, and perhaps early marriage as well have often blocked many of these parents' path to sufficient education or special training. Difficulty in getting along comfortably with others may make it hard to hold a job or friends. It is not at all uncommon to hear that a young father has had a hard time keeping jobs because he gets into a fight with each boss in turn. Many abusive parents are impulsive, or have trouble in problem solving and thinking ahead, so that simple problems are made far worse by the way they try to cope with them. Budgeting, taking advantage of opportunities, using the community help to which they are entitled, are not part of their lifestyles. We know that child abuse is most apt to occur during a time of crisis; the loss of a job or a fight with the landlady may be just enough to make the crying of a teething baby unbearable.

Still, there are, of course, also abusive parents who are successful at work and do not suffer from financial or housing crises. But these too suffer from crises in relationships. A fight with a mother-in-law can occur in any income group and can result in exactly the same feelings of being criticized and rejected. Babies teethe in all income groups as well, so that the basic crisis will be the same and, given the same potential for abuse, so generally will the outcome. For the well-to-do the situation may be helped by a nursemaid or babysitter who looks after the baby when he is fussing. Yet it is surprising how rarely these parents avail themselves of hired help. They usually insist instead that they should and can care for the baby all the time.

Perhaps part of the problem is that abusive parents do have trouble turning to others for help, in trusting others to *want* to help. They tend to be isolated, without friends and without confidants. In a crisis they seem to feel they must struggle alone; asking for help represents failure. It may well be that, just as children they accepted their parents' unrealistic expectations of them, now as adults they have unrealistic expectations not only of their own children but also of themselves. They must prove their ability to care for their child, no matter what the cost to him. Abusive parents seem not only to retain their own parents' ideas about child-rearing, but they also seem, even as adults, unable to disagree with those ideas and act independently. We are constantly struck by the eagerness with which abusive parents we have observed look to their own parents for approval in everything they do, and by the intense disappointment and anger they feel when they are criticized instead. No matter how much they have resented the way they were cared for by their parents, only too often they look for approval by repeating the pattern for the benefit of the grandparents.

When a child is abused, it is always at a point of crisis, often an apparently trivial one. The infant's interruption of its parent's sexual intercourse by protracted crying at night is a common source of crisis, but the most frequent irritants are messy feeding, soiling (particularly when a parent's clothes get soiled), and intractable crying. One young woman described this incident with her two-year-old girl: 'I don't know what happened. I felt just fine – no worries – and suddenly when she couldn't get her body shirt undone and peed on my freshly waxed floor, something snapped, and I threw her across the room as if she had killed somebody or something.'

Many parents have told us they see persistent crying as accusatory. An abusive mother will regard a crying or fussy baby as hungry or wet or full of gas. She will proceed to do all the obvious things to help the child, but if everything fails she will try harder and harder to pacify him until, in a moment of utter frustration, she is overwhelmed by the thought that the baby, even at two weeks of age, is saying, 'If you were a good mother I wouldn't be crying like this.' It is precisely because the parent tries to be extra good, to be loving and earn the love of the child, that intractable crying is seen as total rejection and leads to sudden rage. The abuse is clearly not a rational act. It is not premeditated, and it is often followed by deep grief and great guilt. Such parents are seen by doctors and nurses as being very solicitous. Third parties find it hard to believe that so loving a parent could have inflicted such serious injury.

## FACTORS THAT ADD TO STRESS

In addition to the main predisposing factors, others that can have an effect on background stress are the intelligence of the parents, the state of their health, their socioeconomic status, cultural background and psychological make-up. The handicap of low intelligence makes it difficult to cope independently in a competitive society; parents need to have knowledge and good judgement to care for young, helpless children. When the parent's lack of ability is combined with emotional difficulty and impulsiveness, the child is in danger. A mentally slow mother of four children took in a boyfriend who beat her and severely abused her children. She was so intimidated by his threats that she was afraid to go to the authorities, but was relieved when, after six weeks of abuse, her mother did.

Chronic illness may make it difficult to provide economic or even physical care for a child, no matter how much the mother may wish to do so. A mother blind from birth, for example, needs help in encouraging her child's development in those areas where vision is important – such as providing early visual stimulation by interacting face to face and smiling.

When a parent's cultural background is very different from that of the community in general, this can naturally lead to a feeling of estrangement. The simple fact of isolation may make one cling even more to the old values, seeing their loss as a threat to one's very identity. When the cultural values include unaccepted child-care practices, parents may resent and strongly resist any attempt to change them. A father may cling to the disappearing evidence of his masculine authority and react with fury beyond reason because loss of familiar authority represents for him the loss of much else. In another culture, a potentially dangerous situation could be defused by the appropriateness of the parental demand. For example, a strict father would need to assert his demands less aggressively if the surrounding community agreed with him that his daughter should not date until seventeen.

The enervating effect of continuous poverty and the helpless frustration of social discrimination undeniably contribute to lifelong patterns of failure. The interrelationship of these factors with abuse, and even more with neglect, are close, but the cure does not lie simply in offering money and social opportunity. These factors are connected so that the effects of a brutalizing or emotionally deprived childhood lead to a disordered life pattern, and then to economic and social disadvantage. The problem of social ills may owe as much to individual and family pathology as to the broad social framework in which the family has its place. Solutions are likely to involve not only broad economic and social reform, but also treatment of the individual family.

Among two-parent families, there is generally one parent who is the active abuser, or more strikingly neglects the child, and one who acts as an accessory by arranging for, condoning, encouraging, or covering up the abuse and neglect. Lack of awareness of serious problems between spouse and child, sometimes leading to obvious physical injuries, appears occasionally to be the result of some unconscious block; if so, it must represent a great capacity for denial. In such a family, maintaining the marital relationship seems to be the first priority. Child abuse is indeed a family affair. In our experience, single parents are rather less abusive than couples, which is surprising because one would think that a spouse would provide support in the face of crises. In fact a spouse who is not supportive is worse than no spouse at all when it comes to childrearing.

And spouses are generally not supportive in abusive families; each looks to the other for help and, meeting only a counter-demand for attention, is apt to take out the disappointment in criticism and antagonism. Instead of trying to be helpful in finding ways to care for their children more successfully, each is apt to disavow any involvement or to criticize, leaving the other feeling more helpless than ever. A wife very often stays at home with her child all day; as soon as her husband returns tired from work, she greets him with the demand that he do something about this terrible son of his. 'You're the man of the house! You do something!' Challenged not only as father but as masculine authority, he hits out. He may know nothing else more effective.

Likewise, the mother who has tried for hours to quiet a crying baby may hear her husband shout, 'Can't you keep that damned kid quiet? How can I go to work tomorrow if I can't get any sleep around here?' It enrages her that he does not recognize the prolonged efforts she has been making and that he assumes all the responsibility is hers; she takes out her accumulated anger on the baby.

For abusive parents, feelings of helpless frustration and aloneness are compounded by a general lack of child-care skills. These can be learned, but such parents do not know of their existence and are often resistant to the whole idea of learning.

Child abuse occurs in the presence of four factors. We have just examined three: (1) the parents must have a background of emotional or physical deprivation and perhaps abuse as well; (2) a child must be seen as unlovable or disappointing; (3) there must be a crisis. The fourth factor is that no effective 'lifeline', or line of communication to sources of aid, exists at the moment of crisis. This factor is most important. Lifelines to call for help are essential to all of us. Since abusive parents cannot rely on each other for rescue in moments of crisis, outside lines have to be developed quickly in treatment. Clearly, one cannot easily change parents' emotional backgrounds or twenty-year histories of deprivation, nor can one help them to see their children as loveable; but one can provide for rescue and the beginning of crisis management. We will consider such provisions in some detail in the second part of this book.

# 3/The Abused Child

As parents vary, so do their children. Even within the same family, children differ greatly. Each child has his own unique significance for his parents: he may be their first experience of parenthood, or he may perhaps arrive handicapped in dreadful contrast to a healthy firstborn.

Sometimes in the first few moments after birth the baby's sex, or some aspect of his appearance, will produce in his mother a whole constellation of expectations about what he will mean to her. If he looks like his parental grandmother, just because he has reddish hair, his mother may credit him with all the critical meanness and selfishness of her mother-in-law. Once a notion like that has been entertained, it may reinforce unconsciously the perception that the baby, when he cries, is also being critical and selfish. This may seem farfetched, but many a mother, seeing her son at birth, has sighed with obvious feeling, 'He's just like his father – it's sickening!'

Problems that arise as a result of a newborn baby have generally a much more practical origin. The work of Margaret Lynch has emphasized how a mother's illness during pregnancy, a prolonged and difficult labour and delivery, congenital malformations, or birth injuries (particularly those resulting in brain damage), and prematurity, with its uncertain outcome and disruption of hopes, are all associated with increased potential for abuse. Separation of the baby from the mother because of prematurity or illness, or of the mother from the family through illness, creates further stress.[1]

There is a widely held belief that abused children or those failing to thrive are not lovable, that it is the primary factor in the child-abuse equation. Like so many other theories in child abuse and neglect, this one does account for some cases, but only if there is no other problem in the family background.

Ideally, a wanted child is regarded as lovable by both mother and father; they support each other and are delighted with their roles as parents. The baby quickly responds to cooing, stroking, cuddling and talking, and at an early age forms very specific responses to father and mother and a different response to strangers. A baby who can meet his parents' needs, who is undemanding, easy to care for, healthy, and to them attractive will add to the positive feelings they already have and increase their attachment to him – and vice versa. Many babies can even delight parents who, to start with, find babies only very mildly attractive. But some children are, right at birth, perceived by one parent or the other as simply so different from prior fantasy that their perfectly normal newborn behaviour, such as soiling and crying, is regarded negatively, and no bond of love develops. And if the infant is premature, small for gestational age, ill at birth, has some inherited defect that makes him imperfect, or is not cuddly but stiff and unresponsive, a disastrous relationship can develop. The child is a disappointment and is let known that he is. Whether he was 'lovable' or not in the first place, he quickly becomes to the parents a veritable monster, and bonding in hate may result.

Some children are genuinely difficult to care for, but receive the most loving, patient, and selfless care from their parents and siblings. There are children with obvious physical anomalies, such as hare-lip and cleft palate, that interfere with simple feeding. There are seriously retarded children whose inability to smile, stiffness, or spasticity prevent them almost totally from providing the parents with the rewarding response needed to build and enhance a good relationship. The birth of a defective child is always an enormous shock to the parents and they go through a reaction of denial and grief and anger, but it is remarkable how many correctable and even uncorrectable serious congenital defects are accepted by families with compassion. Rearing a handicapped child is undeniably difficult. These children may not seem very obviously lovable to strangers, but many are indeed loved, often fiercely, by their parents. Just as it is wrong to say that poverty itself or poor housing or unemployment is the cause of child abuse – ignoring the fact that many millions of poor people do not abuse their children although they live in conditions of deprivation – so it is wrong to assume that a child will be abused or neglected because he cannot easily be loved. Many children become unlovable as a result of having had exceedingly little love offered to them, of having known a life of bare survival or utter hate. Their scars are deep at an early age.

Another very important factor needed to induce a bonding of love is the 'fit' between those characteristics of the baby usually called 'constitutional' and the imagined characteristics the parents were hoping for. An infant who is very placid, sucks efficiently, and sleeps most of the time between feedings is going to please almost any parent. But a baby who seems floppy and lackadaisical when nursing but becomes tense, irritable, and inconsolable when he should be falling asleep can be a trial to the most secure mother. T. Berry Brazelton's work has shown us that newborns' characteristics can be an indication of their adaptability in the early months of life.[2] Descriptions by Alexander Thomas and Stella Chess of various constitutional types also reinforce the view that babies do differ physiologically and cannot all be treated alike.[3] This matters, since caring for a baby is a twenty-four-hour-a-day job, and the caregiver's resistance and patience do wear out. A baby who does not cuddle, but arches back and struggles, may upset one mother if she sees it as rejection, but not another, for whom it may be a sign of strength and independence – portent of the football star. Given the sensitivity of the potentially abusive parent to the early characteristics of his child, and his undue readiness to attach long-term significance to them, it is easy to see how the stage can be set for difficulty and how little outside stress may be needed to create the first small crisis.

## WHEN STRESS BEGINS

Development, both of the baby and of the baby's relationship with the parents, may progress well at first. The time when problems begin depends, largely, on what the parents can cope with. If what upsets them is to hear the baby cry, trouble will start early, for it is a rare infant who does not cry in the first few months of life. If a father is very intolerant of crying and puts pressure on his wife to prevent it, she can become more and more anxious as the difficulty of maintaining constant peace increases. Her anxiety will be reflected in her tense handling of the baby so that he too may become ill at ease. Eventually the crying will break forth unchecked, and either father or mother will reach a breaking point and have to stop it at all costs, usually by smacking and injuring the baby. These early injuries need to be taken seriously, for not only may they do extreme harm to the developing child, but they warn us of very severe disturbance in the parents.

Most often during the first three years it is the normal developmental milestones, poorly understood and accepted by the parents, that account for most of the trigger crises in battering. Crying seems to be by far the most upsetting behaviour, even though it is just the normal way the baby signals his need of attention. For many abusive parents, crying rouses intolerable anxiety and must be stopped. Perhaps these parents, who can rarely cry themselves, are put in touch with the long buried and intolerable desolation of their own early childhoods.

When the baby is difficult to feed, rejecting the bottle or spitting up, an insecure mother may overreact, as if the baby's problems were a deliberate attempt to frustrate her.

Toilet-training accidents are probably the second highest immediate cause of abusive attacks and, along with other normal autonomous behaviour, seem to produce the greatest frustration in the parent who feels he can't maintain control. It is the feeling of helpless lack of control that so often leads to ~age and striking out.

Some mothers and fathers can adjust very well to a baby, provided he is young and helpless, especially if he is also readily comforted by the bottle. One mother we knew had, by the age of twenty-seven, nine children and refused the thought of any kind of contraception. Severely deprived herself as a young child, she had begun to have children as a teenager and lost the first three because of serious neglect. After her marriage to a fatherly man, she had six more, and only when two of them were taken to the hospital for abuse did the plight of all her children come to light. As a baby, each child was welcomed and fed copiously, just as the mother fed herself. She found in food, and in feeding a dependent baby, much pleasure and relief from her own feelings of deprivation. However, as soon as her children could walk and required more attention, care, and management, she began to act towards them as a helpless sibling might, she made no effort to teach them cleanliness or self-help, to control their wild play, or to impose order on the chaos. When she became angry at their unwillingness to conform to her wishes, she resorted to physical punishment – some of it serious, as indicated by her four-year-old son Jack's burn scars, his two fractures long since healed and two new ones, and his short stature. Jack's three-year-old sister also had a black eye and a fracture. A study of the children in this family revealed that the newborn baby and the one-year-old were both well cared for and that the one-year-old showed no developmental delays beyond a lack of readiness to walk. The two-year-old Mary, however, was severely handicapped – almost totally unwilling to walk although she could do so. She spoke only three or four words, and sat for an entire hour in her play nursery with eyes downcast, unmoving. Her expression lightened briefly from its stolid depression when we encouraged her to play peek-a-boo, but never did she smile or look at her companion. Nor did she seem able to play with any of the toys, beyond manipulating them briefly and making one attempt to feed a doll with a play bottle, an attempt that almost immediately deteriorated into poking the bottle at the other toys. Her three- and six-year-old sisters and her four-year-old brother were also suffering from neglect, apparent retardation, and severe emotional disturbance. Severance of parental rights for these older children was obtained, and follow-up reports of Mary and Jack have indicated remarkable improvement. This outcome is important, because it demonstrates that even a child as severely handicapped as Mary can respond to an environment that recognizes her needs and, in another family, can make up many of her developmental delays. Mary is now said to be functioning as a normal child in her adoptive home. The outlook for Jack, who was exposed to abuse and neglect far longer, will become clear less quickly; his progress, although rapid, may never allow him to catch up completely.

## EARLY SIGNS OF TROUBLE

The earliest evidence of neglect is usually the failure-to-thrive syndrome, which is found most commonly in the first two years of life though it can continue throughout childhood. The child failing to thrive, emaciated, frantic, and difficult to cuddle, is easy to distinguish from others with different feeding problems because in the hospital he eats voraciously.

Although we have seen many abused and neglected children of different ages, few clear-cut characteristics have emerged to differentiate between neglect and abuse. The very young infant who has been abused may show no psychological or developmental abnormalities; between bouts of abuse he may get plenty of stimulation and positive attention. This inconsistent treatment accounts for the observation, so often puzzling to inexperienced doctors and nurses, that a child may behave positively towards the very person who abuses him repeatedly. Indeed most abused children do look to their parents for love, unless they have lost all hope. They may know no other kind of attention and will usually accept this one as perfectly natural.

However, there is usually early evidence, certainly by the end of the first year of life, of a fairly pervasive deviance in development. Perhaps the sensitivity of a young child's development to deficiencies in his emotional and physical environment initially accounts for rather ill defined developmental delays, which later may be more closely related to the particular experiences affecting him. Certainly delays in the motor, social, cognitive, and speech development are common, at least by one year of age. It is our impression, not yet proven, that much of the retardation observed in abused children is related less to the physical abuse itself than to the neglect and emotional abuse that often accompany it. Slim support for this probability is supplied by observation of those comparatively few abused children who are well cared for physically and given a great deal of loving attention by parents who may see them as unusually good and gifted. Such children may have very unreasonable expectations placed upon them – demands for intellectual achievement (for instance, learning poems or multiplication tables at a very early age) or for unrealistically impeccable manners. So long as the children are able to perform, they are not punished, but if they fail, punishment may be severe. For such children life can be happy, but only so long as they are able to keep up the pace of performance. The message is clear: 'Be good in the certain way that matters to Mummy and Daddy and all is well. If you are not, you have reason to fear.' Some children manage to keep up and may seem to be well adjusted and happy. It is only on closer examination and outside the family that they may be found to have overdeveloped skills in the areas prized by their parents, with much less impressive general abilities. They are also apt to be very anxious and often covertly resentful, for they are well aware that, for them, love is conditional.

This emphasizes an important fact: the symptomatic

behaviour of the abused or neglected child is his way of coping with expectations that are not faced by most children, but are specifically those of his parents. How much attention of any kind he receives and how much he escapes abuse depend on how well his coping style fits these expectations.

The child whose parents are primarily neglectful must adjust to the fact that his mother's and father's needs for attention, love and care come first. When his parents' needs are met, they may be less preoccupied and have time for his own needs for food, cleanliness and cuddling. The mother's distorted perception of her child as insatiable, potentially bad, and a threat of all kinds of future trouble largely accounts for the way she ignores his real needs. What does this do to the child, especially if deprivation starts at an early age? In all likelihood, a pleasurable interchange, such as that filmed so illuminatingly by Berry Brazelton, never takes place.[4] Another film, by Edward Tronick, reveals what probably does happen.[5] In this experiment the mother, after a first episode of warm interchange, leaves briefly and then returns for a second time. Again her baby greets her warmly, but this time she remains impassive and unresponsive. The baby tries again and again, with diminishing vigour, to elicit the usual responses, and finally subsides into what looks like bewildered and immobile distress. If a child meets impassivity, not just for two minutes but for the duration of his contacts with his parents, it may not be surprising that his innate capacity for active, pleasurable socialization is stifled. If he has to compete with others who can meet his parents' interests better or complain more effectively, he may not have much chance of getting attention. If his parents are not only inattentive but liable to respond to his crying or complaints with impatient blows, his lot may be even more precarious, and as soon as he is old enough he will have to exert himself actively to get anything.

Many children's best hope of getting food, attention and care in such a hostile environment seems to be total submission to their parents' wishes. Their anxious attempts to understand what those are may be the origin of the extreme attentiveness of so many young abused children, what Christopher Ounsted calls their 'frozen watchfulness'. These children stare continually, revealing (later when they feel more free to talk) a remarkable memory for physical surroundings and events. It is as if they can take nothing for granted, but must always be on the watch to avoid trouble or to try to please. Their eyes constantly scan the environment for danger, while at the same time their faces are immobile; there are no spontaneous smiles and almost no eye contact. It is as if they think that by not looking someone in the eye they make themselves invisible and therefore safe from attack. These children naturally also tend to be fearful and shy. Avoiding physical punishment may be the best they can do to improve their relations with their parents. They may not have learned how to please with smiling, social behaviour. What they do imitate – hitting or the often-heard word 'no' – may be ignored because it is the family norm, or it may induce punishment because it comes from a child. Thus, all the optimal conditions for learning are missing: sensitivity to and encouragement of innate potential, stimulating opportunities for exploration and exploitation (of mother as well as of toys and ordinary utensils). They are replaced by the adversive conditioning of punishment, particularly for physical initiative or emotional and vocal expression.

Another outstanding characteristic of young abused children is their compliance and acceptance of whatever happens. They are passive and obedient, even when in the hospital they are required to submit to painful procedures, or when in the process of an evaluation they are taken away from their parents by a stranger. They will remain in uncomfortable positions for a long time if asked to do so, or sit quietly while their mothers talk for a long time. That this truly is compliance is proved by their gradual growth of assertiveness and resistance if they are removed to a more permissive environment. There they will eventually react much more normally to people other than their parents.

Young abused children seem stoic at first, expressing no feelings, even of physical pain. It may take days in permissive surroundings, and sometimes plenty of adult encouragement too, before they show how hurt, frightened, or lonely they feel. We have to keep this in mind when getting to know an abused child; he will need time to develop some trust, and he may need to know his feelings are permitted and encouraged before he feels safe to express them. He will also be markedly sensitive to criticism or rejection; early on in a relationship he will usually need only the gentlest of suggestions to try to please. Harshness will cause a quick return to frozen watchfulness and withdrawn mistrust. This anxiety to please does not mean he has no anger in his make-up. On the contrary, the feelings of resentment and fury are only pent up, ready to burst forth in play, sometimes against a smaller child, when it finally seems safe to let them go. One little girl, who suffered severe head injuries, gave the impression that her only wish was to please adults: every sentence was sweetly worded and ended with the upward inflection of a question – no risk of displeasing an adult there! Yet, after some months of the utmost tractability, one could see her bang a doll by its head repeatedly, with unalloyed pleasure. She particularly delighted in having the 'baby' be naughty so that she could punish it in precisely the way she herself had been punished.

One example of the natural history of abused and neglected childhood is provided by Leonard, a baby whose mother had been deprived and had lost her own mother at an early age. Leonard had a robust, well-loved, three-year-old half-brother whose father had been divorced by their mother. Leonard's father, subsequently, had deserted the mother during her pregnancy, and she was upset to find that the girl she hoped for turned out to be a boy who looked like his hated father. Leonard was a healthy baby and, although he did not sleep very well, thrived until he was four or five months old. After that he was not seen in the well-baby clinic until he was hospitalized at thirteen months with severe emaciation and some bruises. At that time it was stated that he had eaten poorly and had intermittent diarrhoea since he was six months old (about the time his mother became pregnant again by a different father). When first seen in hospital, Leonard seemed miserable and severely depressed. He did not look at anyone, smile, or talk; he frowned often (an unusual expression in a healthy child), and was totally passive. He could barely sit and could not stand. He was listless and made no response to his physical examination or injections. Leonard was voraciously hungry and would cry and protest feebly when the bottle was taken away. Aside from having to restrict his feeding for three days because of starvation diarrhoea, our only special treatment was to provide him with a 'foster grandmother' (one of the retired persons who provide invaluable service in the hospital by giving close personal attention to small patients in need of individual relationships). After ten days, Leonard was pushing himself about in a stroller, and was still eating whenever allowed and beginning to gain some weight. He had lost the anxious, frowning look he first had. He had developed a loving relationship with his foster grandmother, very satisfying to both, and felt secure enough in her encouraging presence to assert himself and indicate his wish to feed himself. But he was still acutely fearful and sensitive to criticism; when his foster grandmother commented that he enjoyed a young researcher who had made friends with him, Leonard looked sad and backed off. His foster grandmother reassured him and Leonard was able then to smile and play with both. Leonard's mother had made few and cursory visits, and by the time of his discharge had decided to relinquish this unwanted child and look forward to the end of her pregnancy and her remarriage instead. For Leonard, this story had a happy outcome, for he was freed from an unwilling parent to find a good adoptive home at an age when he could make a good recovery from a traumatic infancy. Knowing that many of the children who have been adopted at his age in the past have done well and that many of them were unacknowledged abused children, there is reason to hope that Leonard's future should be good.

## 'DEMON' SYMPTOMS

Not all children who have been abused are compliant and anxious to please. At least one fourth of the young children (and more, we suspect, of the older ones) are negative, aggressive, and often hyperactive as well. These children seem veritable demons, who have responded to the experience of aggression with almost manic activity. They move constantly, unable to stand still or attend more than briefly, and are almost completely incapable of playing acceptably with other children. This behaviour may be an imitation of the aggression they have experienced, but it is socially so insufferable that they may constantly be rejected in nursery school or any other play group unless a special effort is made to modify their behaviour.

These are very difficult children to manage, not listening to directions, impervious apparently to disapproval, and forever hitting out at other children. The only attention they seem to try for is negative, and their language is often even more aggressive than their behaviour. Sometimes their hyperactivity seems severe enough to be neurologically determined, and to require medication such as methylphenidate, but more often they seem just to be suffering from disorganizing anxiety and they respond well to a very calm, highly structured environment. One has the impression that some of these children come from a background of chaos and uproar in which they feel totally at sea, and that they look on aggression as the only outlet. Indeed, there are homes in which the only acceptable verbal expression of any feeling, whether anxiety, indecision, pleasure or anger, is an aggressive outburst – a relief of tension within a limited emotional repertoire. It is important that children who have learned only this negative and action-oriented mode of coping be offered some kind of treatment, for otherwise they will not be able to relate to anyone satisfactorily and will become progressively more disturbed. Especially, they must learn how to recognize their feelings, tolerate them and express them verbally, so that their communication does not continue to be primarily an aggressive act. This at least will give them a chance to relate to adults and other children on a more realistic level, and to arrive at the possibility of compromise and rapprochement.

Some children we have treated are practically incomprehensible: at times sweet and compliant and at other times disruptive or impulsive without apparent provocation. One cannot generalize about these children, but it is possible that they are facing the problem of developing an identity, which for abused young children can be very difficult. One little girl, three-year-old Betty, worried everyone with the variability of her behaviour. It seemed that her ability to distinguish reality from fantasy might be seriously impaired. When we observed her closely it seemed apparent that her mother was functioning in a borderline psychotic state and often spoke to Betty and treated her as if Betty were the mother and not she. Both lived in a state of considerable confusion, moving from their own temporary apartment to the grandparents' home to a boyfriend's home. Both father and boyfriend were irregularly at home, and the grandparents were almost daily involved. Each of these people might at any time be kind or abusive or neglectful. When we noticed, therefore, that Betty spent a play hour in role-playing, alternating rapidly between little girl and mother and that in each role she sought to find out what to expect from husband, father, mother, daughter, it seemed clear that all of her energies were occupied in trying to make sense out of chaos and to learn what to expect from the unreliable adults in her environment. It is difficult to form an identity when one has no reliable models.

Abused children have great difficulty in recognizing and talking about their own feelings – especially liking, loneliness, anxiety, and pleasure. Few can allow themselves pleasure and joy, and simple fun and laughing are rare at first. They take little pleasure in themselves either; usually they think of themselves as bad, unlovable, and stupid. They expect much of themselves in one way – in the matter of doing the right thing – but very little when it comes to pleasing and arousing real interest.

Undoubtedly related to their poor self-image is the punitive behaviour some older abused children show; it is not surprising they find it difficult to have fun. They are very quick to find fault with other children and like to prescribe severe punishments, but they are often worried about justifying their own behaviour and rationalize their own wrongdoings. It is possible that they have that very rigid, but at the same time weak, kind of conscience which concerns itself with the forms of behaviour but not its moral significance.

Children can be very preoccupied indeed with the bad picture of themselves. One little girl of three, bright but with some speech difficulties, would play for several minutes at a time, using the play hour well and happily. Then she would suddenly burst forth in a loud, angry voice, repeating a small dialogue vignette in which parents (her own) scolded a child (herself) for asking for food or for minor wrongdoing. Occasionally she said also, 'We won't sell you.' It was discovered that her parents, who indeed saw her as a bad and stupid child, did tease her with threats to sell her; a month after this they very suddenly voluntarily relinquished her.

One boy of six, seen after he had been severely beaten by his stepfather for soiling himself, spent the entire hour acting out and talking about three themes. The first was the violence he saw filling his life, from the boys he regularly had to fight at school to the dangerous dogs he encountered on the way home and the excessively violent and gory movies he saw with his parents. The second theme was his guilt and feeling of responsibility for getting his father into trouble; if he had not soiled himself, his father would not have had to punish him so often. He said, 'My daddy didn't want to punish me, but he had to because I messed my pants. He sort of liked to punish me when I did it and although he didn't want to, he had to because I was bad. It was my fault that he had to and when I go home I'm going to give him a present to make him feel better.' The third theme was his wish to please his parents in any way he could, by giving them presents and magically making all their wishes come true, if only he could go home.

Studies have seemed to indicate that some older children are depressed to the extent of committing suicide, because all their lives they have received the message that they are a burden. Whether or not this actually happens, it is certainly true that there are many younger children who are struggling to accommodate the clear message that they are unwanted and worthless. The strength of this message, when the child is an only child or when he becomes the family scapegoat and his brothers and sisters join his parents in devaluing him, can be overwhelming.

After abused children have been in therapy for some time, they begin to regress during the treatment hours. In such a permissive environment it is not at all unusual for a five-year-old to suck a baby bottle or pretend to be a very demanding baby who wants to be given everything in sight. A useful medium for expressing regressive feelings is water play. Washing is an ostensibly very clean activity which in fact can involve much messy spilling; when he finds this safe, the child can go on to other messy play and freely express unresolved conflicts about the cleanliness, neatness, and toilet training which were required of him prematurely.

As they become more confident in therapy, abused children do learn to express themselves verbally or in play. Then the extent of the anxiety, the fears, and the anger they feel under their quiet manner becomes obvious. For many of them the world seems fraught with all kinds of potential danger, and representations of violence, loss, and separation involving themselves or their family almost inevitably dominate their play. It is not unusual for play hours to be filled entirely with aggressive play, week after week. As they play they may voice their fears directly, and indeed for many of them the reality of their chaotic home situations is not far from the traumatic events of their fantasy.

## A LACK OF TRUST

The older children we see (those over three) seem to be very clearly continuing the distorted course of development the younger ones have begun. They all find it difficult to trust adults, and sometimes other children as well; this lack of what Erik Erikson calls basic trust persists even when they seem to be developing a good relationship, for instance with a therapist. They relapse only too easily into distrust at the slightest sign of disappointment. But at the same time they go on being hungry for nurturance, whether offered as attention or as food or candy. They tend to be greedy for candy or presents and are eager to take away tangible evidence of regard.

Abused children often continue to find relationships very difficult, even beyond the question of trust. They relate indiscriminately, quickly making superficial friendships but ready to discard them at the slightest sign of rejection. They come eagerly to treatment hours, but when the time is up they seem unable to deal with separation and quickly depart as if there were no next time. It seems to us that their early experiences have made it hard for them to acquire what is called object constancy – that is, the ability to see the people they love as always in existence and always basically the same no matter what. With these children it seems to be 'out of sight, out of mind'. They may ignore the therapist if someone else comes along, as if one could not have two relationships at the same time (which in their home experience may be true). Especially revealing may be their relationships with their parents in the hospital, clinic, or before or after appointments. They and their parents often part with not even a glance or a word. Parental greeting may take the form of remarks about behaviour: 'Were you good today?' 'Don't forget your coat again.'

Without treatment between the ages of three and six, earlier behaviour patterns continue but in more exaggerated forms.

The aggressive child remains hyperactive and difficult to manage, since he does not readily respond to restrictive limits and he has not learned to communicate his needs in an acceptable way. The conforming girl grows compulsively neat, shows little spontaneity or fun in play, responds to tests with great anxiety but poor performance, and requires constant reassurance in all activities because she is so fearful of failure.

Even with what seems to have been good treatment through a therapeutic playschool and group treatment for his parents, one little boy we knew still suffered at five from the problems we noted at three. At this age Billy had suffered a skull fracture inflicted by his mother's boyfriend. He was extremely compliant, indiscriminate in his relationships, and anxious to please, especially his mother who expected him to do her credit. He became more trusting, confident, assertive and able to enjoy friends after two years in nursery school and after acquiring a new stepfather. However, six months later, having a demanding kindergarten teacher and parents now more preoccupied with their marital adjustment, Billy was depressed and working below his ability. He had formed a highly exaggerated impression of what he must do in order to win approval and felt both hopeless and resentful. Billy showed us how continued follow-up is important. Kindergarten had proved too stressful for him to maintain his newly acquired gains in preschool.

## BEHAVIOUR OF SCHOOL-AGE CHILDREN

One hears comparatively little about the children of school age who are neglected and abused. It is true that they are less at risk of life-threatening injury, because their bodies are less vulnerable and they can run away or seek help. Yet the children who seek help in school are comparatively few, and the injuries picked up are usually accidentally noticed by alert teachers. A school-age child will often seek to cover up for his parents by fabricating stories of how he got his injuries, but their nature usually gives the real cause away. Abused school-age children and adolescents are often most secretive about their plight for fear of breaking up their families and because they do not see how change is possible. They cover up bruises by wearing clothing that may be inappropriate to the season but keeps the secret and, if they are involved in sexual abuse at home, they rarely tell anyone because they cannot imagine what good could follow from doing so. These children tend to be lonely and friendless; they already show the same absence of joy and spontaneity as their parents. They may yearn for substitutes to love and often make great efforts to find a friend among youngsters of their own sex. But these attempts tend to fail because their demands are excessive and are not understood by the friend or his parents.

It is distressing to note how often, by the time a child has reached school, he has accepted his parents' punishment as totally valid and rightful. He is usually very much afraid of getting into trouble and may count himself responsible if he does. He has, by then, incorporated into his own conscience and value system the idea that he is in the wrong no matter what he does, and that his punishment is justified. If it makes him angry, that 'counts against him'. He accepts his parents' discipline as the right way to bring up children, since it is the only way he knows.

Perhaps the main reason that child abuse in school years is not diagnosed as often as it should be is that the children usually show ample evidence of behavioural difficulties. Parents' explanations that they punish their children because they are incorrigible are accepted as quite understandable; that abuse and neglect have made them as they are is generally not considered. This is especially true when the child's behaviour is hyperactive and aggressive or, in more withdrawn children, involves stealing, soiling, or school failure.

If what we know about the development of young abused and neglected children holds true, we may expect them to enter school with distinct disadvantages. There is some controversy about whether older abused children show any intellectual deficits or whether it is only those children who have been primarily neglected who have educational handicaps at a later age. Certainly the developmental delays observed between one and four may be made up at least in part when a child is exposed to the ordered and stimulating environment of school, especially if he finds himself for the first time in an environment in which he is safe and not unduly criticized, and in which he finds he can perform well enough. But some younger abused children find it hard to cope with testing situations, and school success may be beyond them if it makes immediate demands for good performance and expressive ability.

It is our impression that some of the school-age children we know perform well enough to get by, but below their true ability. Faced with a demand, younger abused children are often disorganized by anxiety and resort to all kinds of inappropriate coping styles. Some give up immediately and say 'I don't know' to simple questions they can easily answer, rather than risk disapproval by giving the wrong answer. Others are so concerned with the behaviour of the questioner and his intentions that they cannot attend to the task. Others use all kinds of delaying tactics, designed to charm or distract him, apparently in the hope that he will give up or the questions will go away. They have not learned the coping skills that will allow them to formulate the requirements of a task and solve it in more direct and effective ways.

Regardless of their initial intelligence or socioeconomic background, abused children often perform poorly at communicative skills such as reading and writing. Not surprisingly, oppressed children for whom abuse is the reward for expression or initiative have difficulty with learning that requires exactly those behaviours. A child who is over compulsive about getting approval and doing things right will tend to fail because of anxiety, while a child who has learned that communication leads to attention and receiving attention leads to being bashed would prefer to be essentially invisible and inactive. In either case he will not perform well in groups. This helps to explain why it is not only children who have been brain-damaged through head injuries who show poor school performance, but far more often children whose physical abuse has actually been stopped. Intervention may have managed to prevent permanent physical injury, but will not have produced the nurturing home environment that is so important for successful learning.

Adolescents are just as inclined as younger school-age children to cover up parental abuse as a shameful secret. One young father told of his own father's reaction to his coming home late for supper one evening at the age of fourteen; he was choked so severely that despite hot weather he had to wear turtlenecks for several days to hide the bruises at school. He was extremely concerned that no one find out because he would not know how to explain.

If the abuse is severe, an adolescent may run away repeatedly, but unfortunately without seeking appropriate help from the authorities. Many begin to express the anger they have felt for so long, not at home, but in delinquent behaviour elsewhere. Belonging to a gang, which gives such teenagers a feeling of being wanted, can help them deal with their feelings of emotional deprivation and can also become a means of discharging pent-up aggression in group-approved delinquent activity. Brandt Steele and Joan Hopkins made a study of one hundred adolescents brought to a juvenile detention centre for the first time.[6] Of these runaways and delinquents, eighty-four had been neglected or abused before the age of six, and ninety-two had been mistreated or sexually abused in the previous eighteen months. Other studies of delinquent children and violent youthful criminals confirm the strong link between the experience of being abused as a child and subsequent antisocial behaviour. This of course does not mean that most abused children later break the law, but it does suggest that those who do break the law often have a history of abuse.

A considerable number of the runaways admit to being abused at home and to attempting, for the first time, to get

away from an intolerable situation. Before adolescence they
have usually seen no other alternative but to submit; even at
twelve or thirteen to run away is a drastic step. That they do
so this early proves, if proof were necessary, how enormous
are the pressures on an abused child.

# 4/Incest and Other Forms of Sexual Abuse

A discussion of incest and other forms of sexual abuse of children is likely to bring forth strong feelings of revulsion or disbelief among readers. But these are the same feelings that have caused professionals to shy away from the problem of sexual abuse and to underestimate its severity and extent.

In order to make these problems more real and to indicate how they may be dealt with, a number of case examples are included in this chapter. The progress that has been made in understanding physical abuse, which seemed at one time just as abhorrent, has led us to feel that this problem should be dealt with just as openly.

Sexual abuse is defined as the involvement of dependent, developmentally immature children and adolescents in sexual activities that they do not fully comprehend, to which they are unable to give informed consent, or that violate the social taboos of family roles. It includes paedophilia (an adult's preference for or addiction to sexual relations with children), rape, and incest. 'Sexual exploitation', another term frequently used, is indeed apt; these children and adolescents are 'exploited' because sexual abuse robs them of their developmentally determined control over their own bodies; and of their own preference, with increasing maturity, for sexual partners on an equal basis. This is so whether the child has to deal with a single, overt, and perhaps violent act, usually committed by a stranger; or with incestuous acts, forceful or otherwise, often continued over many years.

Scientific studies of the incidence of sexual abuse are even more rare than of physical abuse. Data collection has been impaired by what has been euphemistically called a 'family affair'. In discovered acts of paedophilia, the child complains to his parents about fondling or exhibitionism, the police are involved, and a report is made. The same holds true for child rape. In such situations, data are at least minimally correct. As far as the child is concerned, family and professional support for the victim are strong, and criminal conviction rates are relatively high; paediatricians are often informed early on and participate in the diagnosis and treatment of victims. In instances of nonviolent paedophilia, particularly a single act that involves a stranger, simple reassurance of the child and genuine reassurance for the parents are all that is required. Forcible sexual abuse and child rape involving strangers often call for long-term supportive therapy for each member of the family in addition to the treatment of sexual injuries.

The discovery of incest, on the other hand, finds the family and the community reacting in a rather different way. If the victim makes the report, it rarely results in family support or in successful criminal prosecution. Moreover, it is common for children regularly dealt with by physicians and teachers to be involved in incest for many years without their knowing it. Incest makes professionals, along with everyone else, very uncomfortable.

Some doctors routinely ascribe specific complaints of incest, and even incestuous pregnancy, to adolescent fantasy. Often paediatricians will simply not think of incest in making an assessment of an emotionally disturbed child or adolescent of either sex. Still, a history of incest is so commonly found among adults who, ten or fifteen years after the event, come to the attention of psychiatrists, marriage counsellors, mental-health clinics, the police, and the courts that the failure to consider the diagnosis early on is somewhat surprising. Most of the youngsters we now see are under the care of a paediatrician in private practice or in a clinic setting. They represent the children of professionals and white- and blue-collar workers, as well as the poor, in a way that reflects a true cross section of the community. So does the racial distribution which, contrary to published reports from welfare departments and the police, indicates that no one race in Denver is over-represented in sexual abuse.

Reports of incest now reach 150 per million population per year, but under-reporting is massive. In incest there is often long-standing active or passive family collusion and support. It is understandable that the family resists disrupting the existing relationships: disclosure will result in public retribution, with the firm expectation of total family disruption, unemployment and economic disaster, loss of family and friends for the victim, and probably incarceration for the perpetrator, at least until bail is stood. For each person involved there is also the public shame of failure in his or her role as father, mother, and child, with further loss of self-esteem by all.

The Children's Division of the American Humane Society reported five thousand cases of sexual abuse in the United States in 1972. Since only a small fraction of the instances of sexual abuse are reported at the time they occur, most coming to light many years later, it is our view that the true incidence must be at least ten times higher. In the first six months if this year, the Denver General Hospital alone saw eight-nine cases. Increasingly we are seeing younger and younger children who require urgent care. The group of zero- to five-year-old children has increased in recent years from 5 to 25 per cent of the total, while the incidence during the latency age period from five to ten has remained stable at 25 per cent. Between 1967 and 1972, the number of sexually abused children increased tenfold in our hospital.

Incest is usually hidden for years and only comes to public attention during a dramatic change in the family situation, such as adolescent rebellion or delinquent acts, pregnancy, venereal disease, psychiatric illness, or something as trivial as a sudden family quarrel. One half of our runaway adolescent girls were involved in sexual abuse, and many of them experienced physical abuse as well.

## NATURE OF SEXUAL ABUSE

### PAEDOPHILIA

This form of abuse involves an adult's nonviolent sexual contact with a child and may consist of genital fondling, orogenital contact, or genital viewing.

An example of a good outcome may be seen in the case of Mr T, a brilliant young lawyer and father of two. On several occasions he engaged in genital fondling of six- to eight-year-old girls, friends of his daughter's who were in his house visiting his children. The neighbours contacted us with a view to stopping this behaviour, wanting at the same time to prevent the ruin of this attractive family and to obtain psychiatric help for the patient. This compassionate and non-punitive view was largely the result of their affection for the lawyer's young wife, whom they greatly liked. They insisted, however, that the family leave the neighbourhood promptly. The patient moved to a distant city where he entered psycho-therapy and has had a long-term cure of his addictive paedo-philia. His professional and family life have remained stable.

A less happy outcome occurred for Dr A, a fifty-three-year-old physician, who was accused of fondling the genitalia of his pre-adolescent boy patients. A hearing before the medical board confirmed that he regularly measured the penis of each of his boy patients, just as he would record their weight. His defence was that measurements like these are part of comprehensive care, but the board held that the procedure was not routine anywhere, except when the specific medical problem concerned the size of the penis, as is the case in some hormonal disorders. He voluntarily resigned his licence to practise but refused offers of help.

VIOLENT MOLESTATION AND RAPE

While all sexual exploitation of minors is illegal, when rape or other forcible molestation occurs society is particularly concerned with retribution that will prevent repetition. It is not necessary for hymenal rupture or vaginal entry to occur for the rape statute to apply; frequently, vaginal tears, sperm evidence, or a gonococcal infection can be the ultimate proof, but often perineal masturbatory action leads to emission of sperm outside the vagina, on the skin or the anus. Many molestors experience premature ejaculation and others are impotent. We find sperm less than 50 per cent of the time. Orogenital molestation may leave no evidence, except the child's story, which should be believed – children do not fabricate stories of detailed sexual activities unless they have witnessed them, and they have, indeed, been eyewitnesses to their own abuse.

John S, the twenty-three-year-old unemployed boyfriend of a divorced middle-class mother, was babysitting for her two daughters, aged six and fourteen. He first began to sexually assault the fourteen-year-old girl and raped her, despite her efforts to resist by screaming, hitting and biting. When she ran for help to distant neighbours, he raped the six-year-old and fled. When captured, he told the police that he had had two beers and remembered nothing of the events. Both children required hospital care for emotional as well as medical reasons. The six-year-old had a one-inch vaginal tear, which was repaired. The older child had a hymenal tear and many bruises. Both had semen in the vagina and required antibiotics to prevent gonorrhea, with which the attacker was afflicted. Loving and supportive nursing and, later, psychiatric care were given to both victims, who seemed to view the event as 'a bad accident'. The mother had good reason to feel guilt since she had known that her friend was unable to handle alcohol without becoming violent. His psychiatric diagnosis was 'violent and sociopathic personality, not likely to change at any time', and he remains in prison for an indeterminate sentence; but he is a model prisoner to date, and will eventually gain parole.

## INCEST

It is our belief that incest has been increasing in the United States in recent years, perhaps because of the great changes in family life: rising divorce rates, birth control, abortion, and a more tolerant view of sexual acts between non-related household members who come from divorced or previously separated homes. This is particularly true of brother-sister incest between step-children who are living as a family but are not related; we believe that cultural attitudes about this group of adolescents are rapidly becoming more casual.

Society tends to be more concerned with fathers who sleep with or genitally manipulate daughters or sons than with mothers who do the same to sons or, rarely, daughters. This double standard is probably based on the belief that the sheltering mother is simply prolonging, perhaps unusually but not criminally, her previous nurturing role. It is quite clear to us that mothers who regularly sleep with their school-age boys, refer to them as 'lovers', and sexually stimulate them are very seriously ill; but intervention is difficult because mothers are given enormous leeway in their actions where fathers and brothers are not.

Father-daughter incest accounts for approximately three-quarters of incest cases. Girls involved with fathers or step-fathers are often the first daughters in pre-adolescence or early adolescence. Mother-son, father-son, mother-daughter, and brother-sister incest account for the remaining one quarter.

Father-daughter incest is usually non-violent. However, in pre-adolescence and early adolescence, the association between physical abuse and sexual exploitation is sometimes striking, if rarely discussed, and it is not uncommon for adolescent girls we observe acting out under treatment to suffer from both. We do find men with psychopathic personalities and indiscriminate sexuality who view children as objects, and these men are often violent. But most fathers incestuously involved with their daughters are introverted personalities who tend to be socially isolated and family-oriented. Many, gradually sliding towards incestuous behaviour, are given the extra push by a wife who arranges situations that allow privacy between father and daughter. She may, for example, arrange her work schedule so that it takes her away from home in the evenings, and tell her daughter to 'take care of Dad' or to 'settle him down'. It is not hard to see how a very loving and dependent relationship between father and daughter may result, first, in acceptable degrees of caressing and later in increasingly intimate forms of physical contact. In the silent agreement among husband, wife, and daughter each plays a role and is generally free of marked guilt or anger unless a crisis occurs. One of these crises is public discovery. A daughter, of course, is robbed of her developmentally appropriate sexuality and is often caught in the dilemma: if she ends a now embarrassing affair in order to live a more usual life with her peers she will forfeit the family security that, she believes, her compliance has assured her, her mother, and her siblings. It is a terrible burden for these immature women to carry – and relief may not come until they leave home and try to build a life apart.

Writers have stressed unduly the seductive nature of young girls involved sexually with fathers or brothers, as opposed to the more important role played by mothers. Though all young girls, learning how to be feminine, tend to experiment in seduction a little bit, and safely, within the family, our experience suggests that this normal behaviour does not explain incest, which is not initiated by the child but by the adult male, with the mother's complicity. Stories from mothers that they 'could not be more surprised' can generally be discounted – we have simply not seen an innocent mother in long-standing incest, although the mother escapes the punishment that her husband is likely to suffer.

Why do mothers play such an important role in facilitating incest between father and daughter? Often, a very dependent mother is frantic to hold on to her man for her own needs and the financial support he provides, and sees the daughter as a way of providing a younger, more attractive sexual bond within the family than she can offer. This is especially true if she is frigid, rejected sexually, or herself promiscuous. Parents' rationalizations for incest abound and must be dealt with in a direct manner: 'I only wanted to show her how to do it' or 'he just needs a lot of sex'. In the vast majority of cases of incest, people are caught up in a lifestyle with no easy way out and must avoid discovery at all cost. In order to preserve the family, the members often deny the incest even after it has been discovered and tend to condemn the victim, if she is the cause of discovery. She is then bereft of all supports and has few choices. Far more often, of course, there is no immediate discovery and only after some time does the victim's emotional need bring about a realization of her difficult past.

Joan, an eighteen-year-old college student with many minor physical complaints and episodes of insomnia, freely revealed her anger at her father who, as she left for college, was having an incestuous affair with her younger sister. Joan maintained that she was not jealous, but wanted him stopped; as she said, 'I have given my best years to him to keep us together.'

Her father, a judge, had begun to stimulate her sexually at bedtimes when she was twelve and to have regular sexual intercourse when she was fourteen, often six times each week. Her mother knew of these acts from the start, encouraged them subtly at first and later refused to discuss the matter. Whenever the patient threatened to leave home her mother told her that she kept the family together and that her two younger siblings would be forever grateful to her for preventing a divorce. The patient had no boyfriends, and few girlfriends, and was anxious until she left home to 'have things stay the same'. The mother, in subsequent discussions, appeared scared and angry, denied that her husband, 'an important man in the community', would do such a thing and protested that he was wrongfully accused; she asked that he not be contacted and disowned her daughter as a chronic liar. But the father admitted, in medical confidence, that his daughter was totally correct and that he was, indeed, involved with his second daughter. He entered therapy with an experienced psychiatrist and over the past years has been able to desist from all incestuous relationships. His oldest daughter will not see him, and he accepts this. He blames himself fully, is puzzled by his craving for love from his daughters, and finally blames himself for his wife's frigidity. He is chronically depressed, on medication, and a borderline alcoholic.

Leslie, a fourteen-year-old girl, was seen by the police: when her sixteen-year-old brother was arrested as a runaway, he told them that his father was having an incestuous relationship with his sister. The parents denied the allegation and so, initially, did the patient. But at the second interview, she began to discuss her fears about pregnancy and venereal diseases and, with our reassurance, described her four-year-long involvement with her father, a thirty-five-year-old computer programmer. The patient was placed in foster care but repeatedly ran away. The father lost his job when he was first arrested and, while awaiting trial, attempted suicide. Subsequently, criminal prosecution was deferred and both parents received joint treatment to help their failing marriage and their relationships with their children. Both children elected to remain in different foster homes until they graduated from high school. Criminal charges were eventually dropped and employment resumed. The marriage was stabilized; both children are in college and seem to be on friendly terms with their parents, though they never remain overnight.

Annette, a sixteen-year-old girl, was seen because an unrelated household member, a boy of sixteen, had been treated for gonorrhea and listed her as one of his sexual contacts. She was asymtomatic; her vaginal and rectal cultures, however, were positive, but for a distinctly *different* strain of the gonococcus organism. The remaining members of her large family were then cultured: her step-father was positive for gonorrhea of the same strain, as were her fourteen-year-old and eighteen-year-old step-sisters; throat cultures for the gonococcus were positive in her nine-year-old step-brother, as was his anal culture; her mother's culture was negative. It is likely, but was not admitted, that the step-father, who had a criminal record, had infected Annette since she was not clinically ill and had not been infected by the boy of sixteen who had led to her. The step-father had further infected his nine-year-old step-son and the fourteen- and eighteen-year-old girls. The health department administered curative doses of penicillin to all members found to be infected; noted, wryly, that the initial report of the sixteen-year-old boy was not related to the family infection; and ignored all other implications of this family's chaotic incestuous life.

## AGE OF PARTNERS

In paedophilia or child rape the child tends to be between age two and early adolescence, whereas incestuous relationships may begin at the toddler age and continue into adult life. The median age for incestuous behaviour in recent years has been between nine and ten years of age, well within the age group routinely seen by paediatricians, including those paediatricians who do not attend adolescent patients.

Violent acts of sexual exploitation or rape are usually perpetrated by males under the age of thirty, while father-daughter incest tends to involve middle-aged men between thirty and fifty. Other incestuous relationships, as between siblings, can vary from mutual genital play in early childhood and school age to attempted, sometimes successful intercourse in adolescence. One grandson-grandmother relationship involved a boy aged eighteen and a woman aged seventy. At least three physicians dealt with the emotional problems of her delinquent grandson, but none of them was prepared to accept the diagnosis readily admitted by both patients.

## SUBTLE CLINICAL FINDINGS

Where parents report to the police a single episode of abuse caused by a stranger, a babysitter, a relative, or a household member other than the parents, the diagnosis is usually made before a physician sees the victim. More troubling are those subtle manifestations that are not ordinarily thought to relate to the diagnosis and that must call forth the physician's best diagnostic acumen. Teachers, ministers, social workers, nurses, and others are often able to help the sexually abused child get needed attention.

### THE CHILD UNDER FIVE YEARS OF AGE

Aggressive sexual abuse often results in fear states and night terrors, clinging behaviour, and some form of developmental regression. Here the physician's role is to provide reassurance. In a stable family setting, it is the parents rather than the child who may need continued support, particularly if they do not understand the child's resilience. It may be, of course, that the event will have to be worked through with the child again from time to time, but this can often be done in a nursery-school setting with active support from loving teachers and parents. The child may need further help in adolescence.

### THE SCHOOL-AGED CHILD

In school-aged children, subtle clinical manifestations may include sudden onset of anxiety, fear, depression, insomnia, hysteria, sudden massive weight loss or weight gain, sudden school failure, truancy, or running away.

### ADOLESCENTS

Here, serious rebellion, particularly against the mother, is often the major symptom. The physician who is aware of a specific estrangement between a mother and daughter should consider this diagnosis: girls involved in incest often will eventually forgive their fathers, but rarely will they forgive the mothers who failed to protect them. Or if the physician, teacher, or nurse notices that the daughter has suddenly been assigned virtually all the functions ordinarily performed by a mother, such as looking after the house and siblings, he might consider this diagnosis: parents have reassigned the mother's function to the daughter, in both kitchen and bed. These youngsters must be given an opportunity to share their secret with a sympathetic person.

As children grow older, we often find more serious delinquency, accompanied by a huge loss of self-esteem (obvious in statements like 'I'm a whore', 'I'm a slut'). We see prostitution along with chronic depression, social isolation, increasing rebellion, and running away. There are, on the other hand, some very compliant and patient youngsters who carry the load of the family on their frail shoulders, at great sacrifice to their personal development and happiness. These adolescents are in a terrible dilemma – they are in no way assured of ready help from anyone, but risk losing their families and feel guilty and responsible for harming them if they share their secret. Youngsters may only come to the attention of the health-care system or the law through pregnancy, prostitution, venereal disease, drug abuse, or anti-social behaviour.


## TREATMENT OF SEXUAL ABUSE

We have found through our work that there is a chance, particularly when dealing with non-violent sexual exploitation, to use the criminal justice system to initiate treatment. It is possible to file criminal charges and defer prosecution awaiting evaluation and treatment, provided certain requirements are met:

1. The exploitation must be stopped permanently.
2. Law enforcement authorities must be involved in the plan and agree to the treatment proposed.
3. The prosecuting attorney and the court must concur that the criminal system is not being thwarted; that

rehabilitation is an acceptable course under the supervision, even if remote, of the probation department or law enforcement agency.
4. If the treatment fails, or the arrested adult does not participate, the criminal process will resume. (The legal system can only bypass the criminal process if it foresees a more positive outcome resulting from treatment than from incarceration following conviction.)

Paedophilia may never be cured, but it is often possible to bring all illegal acts under control, as we saw in the case of Mr T. There is no certain cure for the aggressive sociopath who engages in violent sexual molestation and rape. Until we know how to treat such people, we must be certain that they cannot menace a defenceless child. In many cases, imprisonment is the only possibility after conviction, or psychiatric commitment if the molestor is judged legally insane and unable to stand trial.

The treatment of incest, on the other hand, is more likely to be successful and to result in the three desired goals: stopping the practice; providing individual and, later, group treatment for the victim and parents; and helping to heal the victim's wounds, permitting growth as a whole person, including the ability to enjoy normal sexuality. In our experience, it has not been possible to reunite families after incest has been stopped, either through placing the child or removing the offender, unless two conditions have been met: the mother must show that she is willing and able to protect her children; and both parents must admit the problem, share a desire to remedy it, and at the same time either improve their marriage or seek a divorce. Ultimately, treatment can be judged successful only many years later when the child has grown up and is not emotionally impaired.

Projective psychological tests reveal that incest victims see themselves as defenceless, worthless, guilty, and threatened from all sides, particularly by the father and mother who would be expected to be their protectors. Improvement on these projective tests is a useful signpost to progress in therapy. They also clearly differentiate the angry, wrongful accuser from the depressed, incestuous victim and are therefore most useful in early family evaluation when the facts of incest are denied. Favourable outcomes can often be predicted by determining whether the child can forgive the perpetrators, regain self-confidence and self-esteem, and have a better self-image.

A study conducted in Santa Clara, California, reports that 90 per cent of the marriages were saved, 95 per cent of the incestuous daughters returned home, and there was no recidivism in families receiving a minimum of ten hours of treatment.[1] Regrettably, we have been far less successful. In our experience between 20 and 30 per cent of the families have not been reunited, no matter what we have attempted, and we have come to feel that they should not be. Reuniting families should not be the overriding goal. Rather, the best interests of the child should be served. Many adolescent girls do far better as emancipated minors, in group homes, or in carefully selected foster-homes. Once they have broken the bond of incest, society must not condemn these victims to an additional sentence, but provide loving protection and the support of adults who are better models than their fathers and mothers can ever hope to be.

Much less is known about the treatment of mother-son or homosexual incest between a parent and child, but these general observations can be made: like the grey areas of incest, the pre-adolescent's cuddly behaviour with parents is not without danger because, even quite early, children receive cues about their role vis-à-vis each parent, and sexual models can be normal or become highly distorted. After adolescence has begun, guilt, fear of discovery, low self-esteem and isolation all extract a fearful toll. These problems must be faced either sooner or later, and later is generally very much worse.

## PROGNOSIS OF SEXUAL EXPLOITATION

A single molestation by a stranger, particularly of a non-violent kind, appears to do little harm to normal children living with secure and reassuring parents. The event still needs to be discussed and explained to the child. Fierce admonishment such as 'Don't let anyone touch you there!' or 'All men are beasts' are at best not helpful.

After any violent molestation or rape children need a great deal of care. A brief hospital stay, with the mother in attendance, may help to take care of injuries such as a vaginal tear, and also to satisfy the legal requirements for criminal evidence in a setting that is sympathetic and supportive. During an examination, the presence of a mother, sister or grandmother is very helpful. A woman gynaecologist who is gentle and explains the examination, can provide the legally required evidence of rape which can sometimes be used for identification of the offender. At times, children are so afraid and in such pain that an almost equally violent form of rape occurs in the emergency room because of inexperienced physicians and nurses. It is far better to take plenty of time and try to do all that is needed under gentle guidance and among familiar faces.

Incest that occurs *before* adolescence and then stops appears to cause less havoc than incest that continues into adolescence. The principal exception to this is the not uncommon situation where a very young girl is trained to be a sexual object and to give and receive sexual pleasure in order to win approval. These little girls try to make each contact with any adult male an overt sexual event, seeking to initiate genital stimulation. They have, in short, been trained for one profession – prostitution. No problem is more pathetic or more difficult to manage because these girls are far too knowing and provocative to be acceptable in most foster or adoptive homes, and are socially disabled until cared for, at length, by a mature and understanding couple.

Fathers involved in this form of early 'training incest' are not curable, in our experience. Nor is the outlook for the children good, even with treatment, because of the prolonged imprinting inherent in their exploitation.

Incest *during* adolescence is especially traumatic because of the adolescent's heightened awareness and involvement in identity formation and peer-group standards. Frigidity, hysteria, promiscuity, phobias, suicide attempts and psychotic behaviour are some of the chronic disabilities seen in some women who experienced adolescent incest without receiving help. These histories are usually obtained only many years later, and generally the affair has never come to the notice of anyone outside the family.

But boys fare far worse than girls. Either mother-son (or grandmother-grandson) or father-son incest seems to leave boys with such severe emotional insult as to block normal emotional growth. They tend to be severely restricted and may be unable to handle any stress without becoming psychotic. Incest can be overcome – with or without help – by many girls, but it is ruinous for boys. In general, workers agree that early working through of the complex emotions and distorted relationships is curative and that late discovery, after serious symptoms have appeared, is far less satisfactory. The focus of treatment is the family and the youngster must try to build an independent life with sympathetic help from others.

In contemporary society incest taboos are sometimes explained as having no function other than the prevention of close inbreeding, with its possibly deleterious genetic effects. But there are many other reasons to prohibit incest. Margaret Mead feels that where the more broadly based sanctioning system has broken down, the household, marked by reciprocal seduction and exploitation, will fail to fulfil its historic role of protecting the immature and permitting the development of strong affectional ties in a context where sex relationships within the family are limited to spouses.[2]

We believe that *all* sexual exploitation is harmful. This does not imply that criminal sanctions must always follow.

What is clear is that the child may need months of individual or group psychotherapy to come to terms with the event and to integrate the sometimes puzzling, sometimes frightening, and sometimes guilt-laden occurrence back into a normal and secure environment. Here the growing child increasingly assumes charge of his or her control over body and mind. Failure to treat the victims is a far more serious societal deficiency than failure to punish the perpetrator.

# Part II

# Dealing with Child Abuse

# 5/Prediction
## and Prevention

We have seen that the great majority of abusive parents are not monsters but anxious, unhappy people who care deeply about their success as parents and feel great guilt about the damage they do in moments of uncontrollable rage. We also know that if we can manage to reach an abusive parent's memories of his own early life, often deeply buried in self-defence against intolerable depression, we are likely to find there another abused child.

Since the abused grow up to abuse, the intervention and treatment we can offer serve not only to protect children now: they help to break the chain that binds future genera-tions. But clearly what can be done must be done early if it is to be maximally useful. Is there a way we can tell which parents are at risk and need help *before* their children arrive at the hospital terribly injured, or even dead? Based on our studies, the answer is an optimistic yes.

## AN EARLY WARNING SYSTEM

Every time a child is born, obstetricians and obstetric nurses or midwives are on hand to ensure the success of the delivery. They witness the momentous first meeting of mother and baby, and are well placed to observe how the mother, and perhaps the father too, accept the human being they are to care for through childhood and adolescence. Until recently no systematic use was made of what these seasoned ob-servers might have noticed, but in 1971 we decided to classify the evidence from the labour room, and to add to it anything else we could learn about the parents while they were in close touch with the hospital. We set up a study to see whether we could predict, from what parents said and did in the period before and at the time of the birth, those parents who were likely to abuse their children later. If we knew which were the high-risk families, we could have community services set up and focused to provide help as soon as it was needed. After all, it makes little sense to provide excellent obstetric, postnatal, and paediatric care in our hospitals only to abandon the families most in need of help at the hospital door. Without some monitoring service, only chance or unusually strong motivation will bring parents to the professionals who exist to help them *before* enormous damage has already been done.

We made our study of 350 mothers – all fully informed and consenting – having their first or second babies at Colorado General Hospital. To avoid factors that could confuse the issue, we left out mothers of premature babies and of babies needing to be taken from them for intensive care. Our study had two main parts. In the first we set up four screening procedures, scoring parents for factors experience had taught us might be indicators of subsequent abuse. We were interested to see which of these four would turn out to be the most accurate predictor. In the second part of the study we examined the effectiveness of a programme of intervention designed to prevent abuse.

In the initial phase of our study our procedures were as follows. First we interviewed the parents before the birth to discover their feelings about the pregnancy and their expectations about the unborn child. We also asked them what their own upbringing had been like, what their present living conditions were, and how much help they could call on from relatives and friends. We noted what seemed to us a danger signal when a mother seemed to be trying to deny her pregnancy (when she didn't want to gain weight, had made no plans for the baby, and refused to talk about the situation); or when she was very depressed about it and felt great loneliness and fear in connection with the delivery – fear that explanations could not alleviate. Likewise, we noted when the parents said they felt this baby was going to be one too many; or when they themselves came from an abusive or neglectful background; or when they were living in overcrowded, isolated, unstable, or otherwise intolerable conditions; or when the mother's husband and family were not supportive to her and she had no sympathetic friends; or when the parents seemed overconcerned about the baby's sex or performance.

Our second screening procedure was identical to this one, except that a seventy-four-item questionnaire was substituted for the interview.

Our third was to observe the parents' reactions in the labour and delivery rooms. The nurses took notes on what each mother said, how she looked, what she did – and how the father reacted if he was there. Often we made videotapes (with the parents' permission) of mother and child together. The delivery-room staff was encouraged to provide anecdotal information as well about the parents and babies. We counted it as a worrisome sign when a mother responded passively to her baby (didn't touch, hold, or examine him, or talk in affectionate terms or tone about him); or when either parent reacted to him with hostility (spoke in an unfriendly way, looked hostile, or made disparaging remarks about his appearance). We were also concerned about parents who seemed disappointed over their baby's sex, or didn't look him in the eye, or didn't seem to be loving towards one another.

Our fourth and final procedure was to observe the families in the period immediately following the birth and during the first six weeks of their children's lives. This time we noted mothers who avoided looking into their babies' eyes or holding them face to face; mothers who didn't seem to have fun with their babies; who found them too demanding at feeding times, were repelled by their messy feeding, or ignored their demands altogether. We were also concerned about mothers who hated changing nappies, or who are bothered by their babies' crying because it made them feel helpless or like crying themselves. We were also concerned about mothers who, in the hospital, didn't respond to their babies' needs themselves, but handed them over to doctors and nurses; and mothers who disliked other people paying attention to their babies in their presence, and made unrealistic and non-sensical complaints about them. We were worried by parents who continued to be disappointed by their babies' sex; who identified them (by name, looks, or behaviour) with people they disliked; or who spoke about them disparagingly, perhaps expecting far more of them than they could possibly be capable of. We were worried about mothers whose husbands' and families' reactions were very unsupportive or negative, and, still more, about mothers who received little or no meaningful support from anyone at all. And finally we were concerned about husbands who were jealous of their babies' taking up their wives' time, affection and energy; and about families where the older children were jealous – especially if the parents showed no insight into this possibility.

In the end, then, we had four separate and rather long lists of negative reactions or circumstances out of which to create ratings that might be effective predictors of abuse or neglect. Against the negative items we were able to set the following positive ones: the baby was healthy and didn't disrupt his parents' lifestyle too much; they appreciated some likeable things about him and saw him as a separate individual; they were able to rescue him from one another or relieve each other in a crisis; the marriage was stable; the parents could have fun together; the parents had had helpful 'father' and 'mother' figures on whom to model themselves while growing up; they had a good friend or relative to turn to in trouble; they showed an ability to cope and plan ahead, and understood they would need to adjust to the new baby; they had their own home and lived in stable conditions; the mother was intelligent and enjoyed good health; the father had a stable job, was supportive of the mother, and involved with the baby's care; the baby was planned, or at any rate wanted, and the parents planned to use birth control again.

When, some time later, we were able to assess the various measures we had used to predict successful and unsuccessful parenting, we found that the most useful information had been that from the labour wards and delivery rooms: from these data we had made 76.5 per cent correct predictions. The questionnaire alone resulted in 57.5 per cent correct predictions, the prenatal interviews alone 54.4 per cent, and the observations and interviews six weeks after birth 54 per cent. The accuracy of all four measures together was 79 per cent, which is not significantly greater than that for the labour and delivery observations alone. So clearly those are the observations we need to have.

Doctors and nurses working with expectant parents, and with mothers during labour and delivery and after birth, are ideally placed to make sensitive, significant observations of the way parents react to their new babies. Midwives, delivering babies at home, can also use their knowledge of the family as a whole to assess whether they will need extra help. Such observations are not difficult to make, nor is it hard to organize special services and frequent contact for families shown to be at risk. We suggest that such observations should, therefore, become a routine part of *all* obstetrical and post-natal care, just as urine analysis or blood pressure checks for pregnant mothers have been routine for years. If it is only possible to observe a new family once, the best time is soon after the baby's birth, when it is easy to collect observations the medical staff has made during pregnancy and delivery without invading the family's privacy very much. This information gathering will significantly improve every child's chance of escaping physical injury.

## THE VALUE OF INTERVENTION

Although we had to wait months to compile the statistics that would show which screening procedure had been the most accurate and effective, it was possible to use the reactions and responses we had noted to rate the parents broadly according to risk. We selected a high-risk group of one hundred mothers, and a low-risk group of fifty to be used for comparison. All the high-risk parents were to receive routine services without explanation, but only half were to receive 'intervention' designed to counteract what we felt were abusive tendencies. The intervention consisted of close watching and care by a single paediatrician assigned to the family. He would examine the baby in the newborn nursery, talk to the parents in the post-delivery ward, and arrange for the child's first visit to the paediatric clinic when he was two weeks old. Thereafter he would see the child every two months. Additional visits could be made whenever the mother or doctor felt they were necessary. This paediatrician would also telephone the family two or three days after the mother left the hospital as well as every week when there was to be no clinic visit. He could also telephone to check up on any problems that had emerged during a previous clinic visit or telephone call. Whenever he knew that some medical or other crisis was occurring, he would telephone the family again to give them support, and would arrange for weekly visits by a health visitor who knew the background. Where necessary he would refer the family to other medical facilities or to mental health clinics. He could also, if it seemed necessary, call in the help of lay health visitors – volunteers who visit to assess the child's general health, give emotional support to the whole family, and communicate with the health authorities.

For the 'non-intervention' families, nothing out of the ordinary was done after the mother had been discharged, although all the information we had gathered was shared with hospital staff, health visitors and the family doctor or clinic.

When the children were between seventeen and thirty-five months, we made home visits to twenty-five randomly selected families in each of the three groups: high-risk (intervention), high-risk (non-intervention), and low-risk. We interviewed each mother during the visit, carefully observed her behaviour with her child, and gathered medical and social information about the whole family.

At the same time we gathered all verified reports of abuse or neglect of the children from the Central Child Abuse Registry. We included injuries due to inadequate care and supervision, injuries that looked suspiciously as if they had been inflicted, cases of failure to thrive that seemed to be the result of deprivation, and cases where children had been relinquished by their parents, placed in foster care, or kidnapped by one parent. We also listed injuries thought to be true accidents, the reasons given for children no longer being in their natural homes, and data on whether or not children had been immunized. We put all this information together and examined each of our three groups to see whether we could detect any difference between the high- and low-risk groups and, more particularly, between the two high-risk groups.

The results showed, to start with, that we could predict with remarkable accuracy which families were at risk. Of the fifty families we visited in the high-risk group, twenty showed signs of 'abnormal parenting practices' while none in the low-risk group did. Eight high-risk children had been reported to the Central Child Abuse Registry; no low-risk child had. There were three cases of failure to thrive in the high-risk intervention group – the children were below normal weight for their ages and heights. Their failure to thrive was ascribed to deprivation. Two of the high-risk non-intervention children also showed signs of the same syndrome, so altogether five of the fifty high-risk children we saw failed to thrive, while none of the low-risk children did.

In the first seventeen months of their lives, twenty-two children in the high-risk group and four in the low-risk group had at least one accident requiring medical attention. Children in all three groups were equally found to have been immunized, so it seems that even the non-intervention children were getting basic paediatric care. At the age of two, all the low-risk children were still living with their natural parents. Eight high-risk children were in foster care or living permanently with relatives, or had been otherwise relinquished by their parents.

Most significant of all, perhaps, is that no child in either the low-risk group or the high-risk *intervention* group was hospitalized for abuse or neglect. But five high-risk non-intervention children did need hospital treatment for serious injuries. These included a fractured femur, a fractured skull, barbiturate poisoning, a subdural haematoma (haemorrhage on the surface of the brain), and third-degree burns. Only two of these five injuries had been reported to the Central Registry.

Although the interventions in our study did not change abnormal patterns of parenting (only intensive treatment could have achieved that), they did stop children from being seriously injured, and surely that must be our first step. Furthermore, the short-term and long-term cost of the five injuries to the state of Colorado has been calculated at $1 million. By comparison the extra cost of our intervention with the treated group was only $12,000.

Other important evidence continues to accumulate. In a study of babies requiring intensive care following birth, all ten children subsequently injured were from a high-risk group comparable to ours, and none at all from the low-risk group. Another study, comparing 'rooming in', which allows mothers to keep their newborn babies at their bedside for most of the hospital stay, with traditional maternity nursery procedures, which allow mothers only limited access to their babies, found a much lower incidence of abuse among the babies who had roomed in. A study in Scotland has shown that health visitors have a remarkably accurate sense of which mothers are doing well emotionally and which badly, but that they tend to discount their judgment and concentrate instead on mothering skills, assuming that mothers in difficulties will come to love their babies or 'manage somehow'. If they would trust their judgment a great deal of child abuse and neglect might be prevented. Because health visitors, who form part of well-organized systems throughout

Europe, have always, in training, focused on maternal skills, they tend to leave 'feelings' to social workers, and are often very reluctant to face up to the fact that a mother is rejecting her child. Situations have been known when a very needy mother has seen both a social worker and a health visitor every week, while her baby slowly starved to death because neither professional was able to intervene effectively.

## DETECTING ABUSE AND ASSESSING RISK

This kind of prediction of parents' problems, far from being 'labelling' or invasive, gives doctors and nurses the opportunity to practise preventive medicine at the highest level. It is absolutely essential to extend it through postnatal care to include consideration of the mother's behaviour with her baby.

However, it is clear that until such obstetric prediction is universal, and even afterwards, all community care professionals, and particularly doctors, need to be on the alert for possible cases of abuse. A doctor should think of abuse every time he sees an injured child, and he should listen very carefully to the explanation the parent gives. No punishment is reasonable if it involves the bruising of a small child. Vague explanations such as 'He must have fallen down' or 'His brother must have hit him' should be treated with suspicion. When accidents are genuine, parents usually know what happened in detail and are prepared to discuss it. Nor do they delay their visit to the doctor.

Children under six months do not induce accidents so a story such as 'The baby rolled over on his arm and broke it' is quite impossible. Nor do children deliberately injure themselves, unless they are psychotic. Some abusive parents show no concern at all about the injury or how it should be treated. Others are extremely distraught and fearful. Either behaviour might possibly be a suspicious sign. Doctors should also take careful note of small babies' failure to thrive. It could be that the mother lacks basic feeding skills, or she could be producing severe postnatal neglect. Water deprivation also needs close attention. The cause might be an error in mixing the dried milk, but severely disturbed mothers do restrict their babies' drinking because they dislike changing nappies.

When a doctor suspects abuse, he should have the child admitted to hospital, telling the parents 'His injuries need to be watched' or 'Some further tests must be done.' He should try not to show anger to the parents and remember that they too are damaged people in need of help. But he should also remember that a child slightly injured and returned home could be killed that same day. While the child is hospitalized, the social services staff can start the process of diagnosis for every member of the family and make arrangements to help them.

Once a child has been abused, medical staff and social workers need some means of assessing the risk involved in returning him to his parents. We have found that the following checklist of factors in the parents' history can predict that risk extremely accurately:

1. As a child was the parent repeatedly beaten or deprived?
2. Does the parent have a record of mental illness or criminal activities?
3. Is the parent suspected of physical abuse in the past?
4. Is the parent suffering lost self-esteem, social isolation, or depression?
5. Has the parent experienced multiple stresses, such as marital discord, divorce, debt, frequent moves, significant losses?
6. Does the parent have violent outbursts of temper?
7. Does the parent have rigid, unrealistic expectations of the child's behaviour?
8. Does the parent punish the child harshly?
9. Does the parent see the child as difficult and provocative (whether or not the child is)?
10. Does the parent reject the child or have difficulty forming a bond with the child?

# 6/Treating Abusive Parents

What can be done to prevent the appalling waste of happiness, health, even life that results from child abuse? Before we go on to discuss this we should explain that talk of treatment only applies to what might be called the norm among abusive parents. There is a group, amounting to about 10 per cent of the total, who are very seriously mentally ill – too seriously, in fact, for any treatment to be possible. For these there is only one alternative – to end the caregiving relationship by placing the child with relatives or in permanent foster care, or by formally terminating parental rights, to be followed by adoption.

This 10 per cent is made up of four groups. The first is that 1 or 2 per cent of abusive parents who suffer from a delusional psychosis of which their abused child has been made part. Some of these may even believe, 'God is telling me to kill my child.' More usually the delusion involves the mother seeing her child as an extension of herself, with no identity of his own at all. For example, we have known a mother to say, 'No, I'm sure the baby doesn't need to be fed yet; I'm not hungry yet.' She was quite unable to distinguish between her own body needs and his.

It should be stressed that the child has to be part of his psychotic parent's delusional system to be *necessarily* in immediate danger. There are mildly schizophrenic parents who can cope with parenthood – with considerable support from spouse and family – and some children can recognize and deal with the psychosis and remain uninvolved. It is therefore not true to say that all children of schizophrenics should be removed for their safety. But in every case the situation needs careful monitoring to make sure the child's immunity continues, since the natural course of the illness itself may change, and the child's meaning for the parent may also change with development. A child perceived as a desirable part of the self when very dependent may become a 'foreign body', alien and bad, when he begins to want autonomy and freedom and is able to say no. And the child of a schizophrenic parent should have individual psychotherapy at some point, at least by the time he is to start school. He will need it to support his growing understanding of reality and his ability to distinguish or resolve the different interpretations of relationships he finds at home and school.

Another 2 or 3 per cent of abusive parents are aggressive sociopaths; that is, individuals with such low boiling points that they communicate only by bashing. They bash their friends, their wives, and their children indiscriminately. They are generally not articulate but react with blind and impulsive rage beyond their control. They may really love their children, but since they cannot control their aggressive impulses, those children should certainly be removed to a safe place. The usual forms of psychotherapy or counselling are very seldom successful with aggressive sociopaths, who rarely respond well to any kind of help except physical control. The prognosis is therefore very poor indeed, and the likelihood of their children's safe return remote. (A group that may be becoming larger as reporting increases includes the parents who are severely and chronically addicted to alcohol or drugs; while under the influence of drugs or alcohol they are not capable of parenting, and successful treatment for addiction often requires such a long time that the child's safety and future would be seriously compromised.)

A further 1 or 2 per cent of untreatable abusive parents are individuals who are frankly 'cruel'; they torture their children in a premeditated, prolonged, repetitive, and often self-righteous way for such infractions as bed-wetting or slight delays in obedience. These people too are not amenable to treatment while their children remain in their charge.

The final 2 or 3 per cent who are seriously mentally ill are the 'fanatics'. This group includes a great variety of people who use religious or other terms to justify beliefs and approaches to child-rearing that to the rest of the world seem clearly and wholly irrational. Unrealistic expectations of children are not uncommon among other abusive parents, but those parents may be quite amenable to reason. The extreme forms of fanaticism, though, must be considered essentially incurable because the parents are not open to suggestions; their beliefs are based on unconscious emotional grounds and are completely unshakable. Whereas any parent is, of course, entitled to his beliefs in a free society, he obviously cannot be allowed to inflict physical and emotional harm on his child, much less, as happens too frequently, to kill him.

These groups make up the 10 per cent of abusive parents who are not treatable. The remaining 90 per cent can potentially be helped, and after subtracting that further 10 per cent for whom treatment is tried but fails, we are left, in Colorado, with an overall success rate of 80 per cent. These families are reunited within nine months and without further reinjury. The parents cover the whole spectrum of psychiatric diagnosis: some show no other pathology besides child abuse. Frequent psychiatric diagnoses among other parents include character disorders (especially narcissistic and passive-aggressive), neurotic disorders, and chronic depression, and also those very difficult conditions known as 'borderline'.

## WHAT IS TREATMENT?

For abusive parents there are two kinds of treatment: the life-saving telephone line or crisis nursery and the long-term therapy designed to help them overcome their own depressing or devastating past histories in order to be able to love and care for their children. Long-term treatment may involve a relationship with a social worker who gives support of a practical and emotional kind, with a lay therapist who enables the parent to trust and feel valued as an individual, or with an analyst or psychotherapist who explores the patient's past in once- or twice-weekly sessions. This course is more complicated and often more difficult for the parent to accept than the emergency treatment. And yet it is clearly here that any real hope of reducing the incidence of child abuse must lie. Parents – and of all parents abusive ones in particular – distrust the exploratory kind of therapy for many reasons. They may feel that it labels them as crazy, that it interferes with their privacy and autonomy, or that frankness about their feelings and their past will expose them to action from hostile authorities. Such therapy demands a level of articulateness and trust on the part of patients that many abusive parents simply cannot achieve. It may also take a very long time, which means that the therapists available cannot hope to deal with more than a small fraction of the potential clients. Besides, psychotherapy is probably not a suitable treatment *on its own* for many parents: insight into one's gloomy and chaotic situation may be overwhelming without practical help in coming to grips with it. For these reasons, all sorts of alternatives to classic psychotherapy have had to be devised to help abusive parents. The fact that so many families do choose psychotherapy, in spite of all the large reasons for not doing so, indicates how strongly they wish to be good parents and how willing they are to do anything to bring their children home and keep them there.

In considering the treatment of the abusive family, the treatment of the parents should be the first priority. Many disturbed parents cannot cope with the idea of their child receiving help while they do not. They will be jealous – reminded of the neglect and rejection in their own childhoods – and may possibly sabotage the child's treatment. This is not to say that the child should not have his own programme; of course he must, and his siblings will need treatment too, but treatment of the parents has to be primary.

All the treatments described here, both short- and long-term, take into account the parents' enormous need for love, acceptance and approval. No treatment can work if it seems rejecting, critical, or unreliable. Parents in need of treatment are immensely sensitive to rejection and desperately need a real long-term relationship with a friendly adult. All kinds of treatment that exist work on this basis, whether they take place in a psychotherapeutic or a casework setting, in a residential programme where the whole family is involved, or in a psychiatric hospital for those parents so ill from drug abuse, alcoholism or psychosis that life outside is not possible.

## THE HOTLINE

The fact that emergency treatment for crises is available can make it much easier for parents to cope with problems. Even when long-term therapy has helped them to understand and to change their behaviour, they may still need the reassurance that twenty-four hours a day, seven days a week, someone is there at the end of a telephone line if things get too much for them. The simple existence of a hotline may lead parents to seek out help at a much earlier stage than they would have without one. The helpers answering hotline calls may be paid or volunteer lay people, but they will be under the direction of a social worker, and they will have had basic training in coping with distraught people on the telephone. They will also have an exact knowledge of the facilities and resources available in the callers' areas.

Responding to a parent's desperate telephone call may involve any one of a number of strategies. It may mean sending out a police car, or saying 'Take yourself and your children at once to a neighbour and then call the police.' It may mean saying 'We'll send someone right away' or 'If you have transport come to the hospital casualty department and one of us will meet you there.' Or if the crisis is less acute, a taxi to the crisis nursery or to a wives' and children's refuge may be the answer. The person who takes the call must note any information he gains about abuse or neglect, marital discord, child behaviour problems, and medical conditions, and pass it on to the relevant social services department to be handled on the next working day. He will obviously log each call – and the social services should report back the eventual outcome of the case, so that it will be possible to judge how successful the telephone response was.

## CRISIS NURSERIES

Crisis nurseries are an innovation, still too rare, in the United States. They are usually sponsored by the social services or by a voluntary organization, and are places to which parents can bring their children when they can no longer cope or when they need a place to leave them while they themselves go for treatment. Telephone workers, social workers, or the parents themselves may ask that a child be taken there. The nursery needs to be open twenty-four hours a day and should be able to give complete care to all children, from newborn babies to five-year-olds. The maximum stay will usually be seventy-two hours and there will be a physical limit to the number of children the nursery can take at one time. Usually it will be staffed by nursery nurses under the guidance of a child-care professional. There should also be a paediatrician available to treat children's illnesses.

Crisis nurseries range from a couple of rooms, with two or three cots and a bed, to a large, well-equipped and well-staffed unit, depending on whether they serve a small town or a large metropolitan area. It is important to have some play and eating space and bathing facilities, because many children will arrive unfed, needing a bath, clothes, and occasionally medical care as well. Most crisis nurseries need at least two people available at all times; that can be expensive, and in some cases licensing is legally complicated: It is much better if the crisis nursery is *not* in an official building, since parents find it difficult to trust a place with obvious physical links with the same institution that may take their children away permanently if they cannot cope. For the same reason, most nurseries keep red tape to a minimum. Of course, they need a certain minimum of identifying and medical information (and if the child shows obvious signs of ill-treatment, a frank – but not frightening – discussion of the need for a medical examination and a report will be essential). But they should concentrate on getting the kind of brief about the child's likes, dislikes and habits that will enable them to make him feel at home. Bringing in a child may be the moment when a parent first feels able to talk about his or her problems, ready to be referred for immediate practical help or counselling. It is crucial, therefore, that the people who meet the parents are sympathetic, warm and helpful.

Most children brought to a crisis nursery are bewildered; they are alarmed both by the events leading up to their arrival and by the strangeness of a new place, and very worried about what is happening to them and to their parents. Especially if they have been hurt, they will feel punished and rejected, and the possibility of losing their parents forever will seem very real. For younger children, comforting and cuddling until they feel safe is desperately important; for the wary older child, calm and cheerful acceptance may help him stay composed while he gains confidence to talk and ask questions. If the child stays for any length of time, or returns repeatedly, he may develop a trusting relationship with one of the workers and begin to behave spontaneously. He may express his need for the attention and approval he has not been getting at home, or display the kinds of behaviour which have been upsetting his parents. Nursery nurses can diagnose some of the child's behavioural problems and watch out for signs of delay in normal development. They can also help him to play with children of his own age, something he may be quite unused to. And they can share their knowledge and understanding of his problems with the parent.

Although crisis nurseries may seem an expensive way of dealing with child abuse, they are much cheaper in the long run than extended medical care followed by foster care or adoption. Few, if any, parents use the nursery as a free baby-sitting service; they are usually too anxious about being judged bad parents or eventually losing their children because they need to use it at all. The provision of a crisis nursery is certainly one of the most effective ways of preventing parents from injuring their children, and the fact that it is safe, reliable and trustworthy can give a parent a feeling of control over what has previously been an unmanageable home life.

In addition to crisis nurseries, a few cities are now developing shelters for 'battered wives' and their children, who may have been beaten at the same time. Modelled to some extent on the programme developed in Chiswick in London, some of the programmes try to provide more extensive help to mothers than just a few hours of safety.

## CASEWORK BY SOCIAL WORKERS

The social worker is the anchorman, or more usually the anchorwoman, in the long-term treatment of child abuse. In the United States every local welfare department has a child-protection department. It has been clear for a long time, though, that social workers alone cannot have enough impact on the problem. That truth is pressed on us in the most urgent way by the fact that most children who die as the result of abuse do so in families already in the care of a social-work department. The problems for the social worker are many. She may see only the mother because during the day the father is at work, although it may be he who is the abuser. She will almost certainly not be trained adequately to deal with the emotional problems of children. She may not know enough about the dynamics of abusive families to recognize the factors that will lead to a crisis. (She may not understand, for instance, the pressures created by a new pregnancy, or the feelings of rejection that stem from her own departure for vacation or another job without plentiful notice and careful preparation.) But the main difficulty is simply that her caseload is far too large to enable her to keep up well enough with her families to be aware of crises as they appear, or to be on good enough terms with them to be told when they do need help. Even if she knows that an abusive mother is likely to try to get her attention in some subtle and disguised way – complaining perhaps about some trivial matter outside the social worker's domain because she cannot come straight to her real problem for fear of rejection – the social worker is just too rushed to co-operate in the relaxed way that is necessary. She may even worry that, if she allows herself to be made responsible for them, the mother's problems may depress and overwhelm her too. An experienced worker knows that most dependent clients need time to grow before they can become more self-sufficient. An inexperienced worker needs the support of her consultant to feel comfortable with that kind of burden and to develop distance from her client's problems. But experience needs time to develop, and today's burn-out rate of exhausted social workers makes this rarer than it should be. When dealing with child abuse, the social worker needs others to work with her.

## HOME HELPS

Home helps are (usually) women trained in housekeeping and family care so they can take over from a mother if she is away or supplement her if she is ill or unable to manage by herself. They may join the family full time for a few days or weeks, or come for a number of hours a week over several months. Those who do the second may be able to act as social workers' ancillaries and help mothers who have trouble organizing their households or co-ordinating the needs of house and children. A visiting home help can develop a relationship with a mother and, if she is tactful and generous, do much to improve her skills. With abusive mothers she will need to avoid taking over too much or offering too much advice; effortlessly bringing order out of chaos does not teach a mother how to do the same – instead it probably reinforces the mother's feelings of inadequacy. The home help has to show respect for the mother's feelings and encourage her interest in the means of change. Occasional casual suggestions are often a good way to get this process started because they can be made to seem those of a colleague, rather than an authority. Informal sharing of knowledge, if it is done without pressure, can be extended to child care if the mother shows interest. Indeed the home help might act very much as a mother would with her own daughter, though she will need great sensitivity and tact.

## LAY THERAPISTS

Lay therapists, or parent aides, are men and women recruited by child-protection agencies especially to devote part of their time to being supportive to and concerned with abusive and neglectful parents, and in effect to act as their friends. The essence of their relationship is that it is not 'professional'; it can cover whatever time and activity the parent wants or needs. It is important that these therapists should originate, if possible, from the same racial and socioeconomic background as their clients because then they are more likely to understand the particular social problems of the clients and themselves provide a better model.

It is important that people chosen to be lay therapists, though they may have experienced problems, should themselves have benefitted from good parenting They must have maturity, some understanding of the dynamics of abusive and neglectful families, and a genuine desire to help. They must have the empathy to understand the problems of the parents they deal with, without sharing them. Their own lives must be rewarding and they must not look to the parents for gratitude and love. Their own spouses and children must be understanding and co-operative too, especially to begin with, when the parents they are helping are in crisis and need them by their side or on the telephone up to twenty hours a week. It is their ability to give parents this time that makes them so much more valuable in daily care than social workers.

A therapist generally finds that the help most valued to begin with is practical help: providing transport to the hospital; helping with an application for low-cost housing; helping one of the parents arrange for and make a visit to the doctor; encouraging them, in fact, to make a better use of the services they have previously mistrusted and avoided. Besides this, providing some entertainment, even lunch at a hamburger place, can make the parents feel less depressed and more befriended.

No therapist can expect an automatic welcome from a family. She may need great persistence to make contact, a firm determination to help and to be accepted at all, and even longer to be accepted as a friend. For a long time she may be warily allowed to sit in the kitchen, making desultory conversation, before the mother is ready to confide anything. On the other hand, she may find herself surrounded by mother, father, and children, all asking in a roundabout way for her attention, and it may be easy to forget that her concern is the parents.

In Colorado, we try to ensure that a lay therapist does not feel responsible for the safety of the children or the quality of the care they are receiving. Whenever she feels worried about them she should have quick access to at least one professional staff member. In this way she can help monitor the safety of the home, but she does not have to report new incidents officially. It is important to protect her position as the parents' friend. The issue of confidentiality can become sticky, unless she has been careful not to promise too much and unless the agency sponsoring her can use other personnel to visit and make the necessary medical contacts or report. It is sometimes worthwhile in a deteriorating situation to introduce other agency people in addition to the lay therapist who can themselves intervene, so that she can truthfully and effectively remain the mother's ally. This may seem somewhat deceitful, but it is important to remember that protecting the children also protects the parents from the consequences of their own impulses, and also that it would be damaging to them to destroy the only trusting relationship they may have.

Because a lay therapist is more a friend than a professional, a successful relationship does not ordinarily have a formal termination but, rather, fluctuates according to need. Sometimes a parent may make increasing and unreasonable demands, in which case the therapist, with the guidance of her professional consultant, will have to set more appropriate limits and perhaps encourage some other kind of professional contact as well. It is not uncommon for a mother who at first was too mistrustful to see anyone to accept later the need for counselling or therapy.

Not all lay therapists should be women. Although men are usually harder to find for the job (because wages for it are low and as a rule men have more direct responsibility as wage earners) they can make very good therapists and are particularly helpful with fathers. Abusive fathers have the same problems as their wives in developing trust and acknowledging their own needs, and sometimes their concept of masculinity assumes recognition of needs or feelings to be a sign of weakness. They can accept understanding of difficulties in marriage, the strain of caring for children, and the worries of earning a living more easily in talking with another man. However, when the therapist is tactful, both husband and wife are apt to compete for his or her attention; he or she must be skilful in apportioning attention and careful not to take sides between husband and wife.


## PSYCHOTHERAPY

Abusive or neglectful parents have usually suffered so much deprivation or trauma in their lives that treatment with some vague goal such as 'making them better able to function' or just 'making them happier,' with an expectation that this goal might be achieved fairly quickly, will leave both therapist and patient disappointed and frustrated. Treatment must be undertaken with specific goals in mind, and, unless one can spend a long period of time on it, these must be limited goals that do not involve uncovering long-standing and deeply buried needs the therapist can do little to meet. It is true that some patients have been very successfully treated by analysis or intensive analytically oriented psychotherapy over the course of years, but these success stories are always likely to be a small minority since so few therapists are qualified to undertake that kind of treatment and by no means all parents are in a position to benefit. In order to profit by such treatment, patients must be capable of introspection and willing to expose themselves to the discomfort of exploring their own painful histories – which means they must be more highly motivated than most. Abusive parents fortunate enough to undergo this form of treatment, though, can be helped to resolve their ambivalence towards their own parents and to see how their own experiences affect their relationship with their children. A successfully treated parent can then dissociate his child from the pathological identification he has unwittingly given him, and see him and treat him more realistically.

In general, however, psychotherapeutic goals have to be more superficial or immediate than this. They must take into account the patient's life situation, his ability to express his feelings accurately, his capacity for change, and his ability to use support. They must also take into account the length of time the therapist will be available and his skill at the sort of treatment that seems to be required. An immediate, practical goal that might be appropriate would be, for instance, helping the parent to relate more comfortably to other adults so that he can develop satisfying relationships and obtain personal support without looking to his children for understanding and comfort. Or the treatment could focus on practical realities and management, without uncovering buried dependency feelings. Or it could set out to change one particular pattern of behaviour, such as the tendency of some single young mothers to involve themselves with one sadistic man after another, exposing their children and themselves to abuse.

Before any kind of therapy begins, a psychiatric diagnosis needs to be made not only of the patient but of the whole family. It is vital to understand the relative strengths of husband and wife, and their interaction, and to see how the emotional balance between them in meeting one another's needs becomes distorted – perhaps involving their child as the target at which tension is discharged. It is usually helpful to involve both parents in treatment if possible, because it is invariably *both* parents who are involved in abuse, and because treating both gives each the same opportunity to grow and adjust to change. Sometimes they can both attend couples' group therapy, while the more deeply involved one (usually the mother) also receives intensive individual therapy.

## MARITAL AND FAMILY THERAPY

Since, as we know, parents are jointly involved in abuse, it sometimes makes sense for two psychotherapists (one of each sex) to work with them together, to sort out how their relationship may be the source of frustrations they vent directly onto the child. In marital therapy both parents can learn how to express their feelings to each other, to listen and respond openly, perhaps for the first time. That can do much to resolve issues that may never have been recognized.

It might seem sensible to take this joint therapeutic approach to its logical conclusion by treating the entire family, and indeed, where the children are old enough, the family sufficiently articulate, and the level of anger in it not too high, that can be done. It is a particularly useful technique in incest cases.

## PARENT-CHILD INTERACTION

One of the most promising ways of working with parents of children in their first three years is by directly observing and changing interactions between parent and child. This can be done when the parents are already receiving successful and supportive treatment themselves. The parents' therapists and those working on the interactions can collaborate very usefully. Information about how the parent was treated as a child will be helpful in understanding his approach to his own children. For example, a young father, left with a two-year-old-boy whose abusive mother had disappeared, found it hard to accept the little child's babyishness, and tended to be rather standoffish and gruff with him. He was worried about whether he would be a 'real boy' once his developmental delays were caught up. When he told his therapist that his mother had dressed him as a girl and kept his hair long until he was over three to make up for the lack of a daughter, it was easy to understand his concern.

Parent-child interaction therapy usually begins by making a complete history of the child's development, the problems that concern his parents, and the methods they have used thus far to cope. The parents, child and therapist may all be together at first in the playroom, so that the parents grow comfortable with the situation. The therapist can at times model for the parents more effective or desirable ways of coping with their child. Specific family situations such as mealtimes may be used for meetings that can deal directly with the problems they usually provoke. Frequently interactions between parent and child or therapist and child are videotaped, so that therapist and parents can run through them afterwards (without the child) and discuss what happened in detail. The therapist can point out what is good about the parents' behaviour, to increase their confidence, and can ask about how they were feeling during problem episodes. In this way, the parents can develop some distance from their own behaviour and their child's, recognizing some qualities for the first time and noticing how they and their child have affected one another. They can also notice causes and effects and discuss alternative ways of reacting. The therapist can encourage the parents to talk about the sort of behaviour they want to promote, and support them in their aims – or else show them that what they want is actually beyond a small child's capacity. He can pass on to them enough knowledge of child development to make their expectations more realistic and their demands more reasonable. If they resist that strongly, their personal therapists can look into the reasons. By a combination of historical material, interactional observation, modelling, discussion, teaching, and re-experiencing the same situations in different ways, parents can be helped gradually to find more satisfactory means of managing their child and will derive more pleasure from success.

Margaret Jeffrey has described some very helpful methods of encouraging change.[1] Her main objective is to reinforce the parents' positive reactions to their child. She gets them to work on improving two-way communication, giving their child positive attention, adapting the house enough to make it easier for him to conform to 'No-no's', setting up expectations and demands appropriate to his age level. And she introduces them to new handling techniques, such as distraction, refusing to raise the voice (as a way of calming arguments), and consulting a list of age-appropriate behaviour before administering punishment (which has the extra advantage of creating a cooling-off period for at least a few seconds). Jeffrey's final technique is to find ways of bringing in other people to help improve the child's behaviour, so as to help the mother see that her child can improve while lightening for her the burden of producing change and reducing her feeling of complete responsibility for his behaviour.

## TREATMENT IN GROUPS

Group treatment, either by itself or in conjunction with individual therapy, can be very successful – especially when the group is one of couples rather than just of individual mothers or fathers. Men, in particular, find groups acceptable because they feel less 'on the spot' when they can use the size of the group to modify the intensity of their own involvement and when there are other men present who can join them in presenting the masculine point of view.

Parents Anonymous is an especially effective kind of group because it is organized by parents themselves. That can be very reassuring to new parents who may mistrust help from official sources (with good reason). Participants in Parents Anonymous groups feel freer than most others to come to grips quickly with their feelings about their children and their daily experiences, and to share them. They are often able to confront one another without hesitation and, having shared the same problems, are less reluctant to admit to feelings they once assumed were uniquely and shamefully theirs. They can also share some possible solutions to family dilemmas with the added authority of having tried them out. These groups are located away from any agency but have access to one professional counsellor who can help prevent the group from precipitating a crisis in a new member who may be psychologically more ill than they recognize, and can immediately follow up any member who seems particularly upset by what has been discussed.

There are many different kinds of groups organized for mothers, fathers or couples. They may be primarily educational, setting up meetings to teach and discuss the information parents need to understand child development and how to cope with the inevitable difficulties of bringing up children. These gatherings can be quite effective, if the participants manage genuinely to become interactive and cohesive groups and are ready to focus on parenting skills. But the members will need other methods of dealing with their individual difficulties, so that they can absorb what they learn in this emotionally charged area. Parents who have very distorted ideas of what to expect from their children often cling to those ideas tenaciously, in the face of all kinds of professional persuasion. The parents' own emotional deprivation makes them resentful of an expenditure of energy to learn about their children's needs. Their ideas of child-rearing are often geared towards meeting their own needs and are therefore not open to intellectual change. For these parents the experience in which the idea originated must somehow be revived enough to be recognized and understood, so that they can bring reason to bear. Otherwise they are apt to talk wisely in their groups about what to do with their children, but then at home, perhaps after a brief attempt to do what seems 'not really right', revert to their own practices, convinced that these are the only ones that work for their particular children.

Other discussion groups exist which are led by two professionals. These groups, when they are made genuinely cohesive and trusting, can be very supportive and allow confrontation between members, in the way that the Parents Anonymous groups do. They have the extra advantage that members often respond to the co-leaders as parents, which helps bring out into the open the early difficulties they have suffered. The two therapists together can also help members with the difficulties they frequently find in relating positively to two people at once, and in reconciling good and bad feelings about the same person.


## RESIDENTIAL TREATMENT

In an attempt to intensify the effect of the various treatments that can be offered, so the child's future can be more quickly settled, a number of residential programmes are being tried. Some of these are limited to single mothers and their children, some include married mothers who come with their children while the father stays at home and visits when he can, and some include the whole family, the father living in the facility with his family but continuing his regular job. The period of residence can vary from one to six months. In Denver the period is three months, and in that time we try to offer a complete range of treatments at the maximum intensity a family can use, following it up non-residentially over a long term.

A residential centre allows us to offer an abusive family immediate care. The child, who would otherwise be in foster care, can live at the centre and spend gradually increasing periods with his parents as they come to reassume responsibility for him. While there, the parents can observe their children being cared for by the professional staff and, without pressure but perhaps with a little informal teaching, can come to adopt better methods themselves. We also use formal parent-child encounters as a means of giving parents individual help with their children. Aside from this, and aside from therapy and a certain amount of straightforward teaching, we encourage social occasions and outings, and help develop skills in homemaking, budgeting, academic work, special job training, or just hobbies.

A residential programme has the advantage of keeping parents and children together, which encourages bonding of formation of ties of love, or else reveals which families are just not going to experience bonding. It also provides psychologists and therapists with an opportunity to learn in detail about life in potentially abusive situations and about how crises are built. But there are disadvantages. The most obvious one is expense. There is also the problem that deprived families tend to regress in residential care, so that it is very difficult for them to resume independent lives at the end of their stay. So our search for practical programmes is likely to lead us towards using the residential centre as a kind of foster home where parents spend as much of their time as they can with their children while themselves continuing to live at home.

A more practical solution which is now being tried is

that of placing the child in a specially prepared foster home where the biological parents and the foster parents develop a co-operative relationship under the supervision and with the therapeutic help of the National Center for the Prevention and Treatment of Child Abuse and Neglect. Foster parents, children and biological parents are all involved in this treatment programme with the goal of having the child returned home in three months or less. Foster parents here act not only as surrogate parents but also as models and much like lay therapists. It is our hope that such a programme can maintain the parent-child attachment while giving the parents some relief at first and an opportunity to receive help with their problems.

# 7/Treating Abused Children

In devising a treatment for an abused or neglected child, we must start with a complete assessment of his difficulties. Physical, neurological, cognitive, social, and psychiatric evaluations should be made wherever there seems the slightest need, and we must be ready to draw on the opinions of a full range of specialists in child care and development in reaching a family diagnosis and treatment plan. It is important that the brothers and sisters of the abused child should also be treated, since they may well have even more severe handicaps.

Before we begin a long-term programme for an abused child, especially if it will involve the co-operation of the parents, it is well to be certain that they too have embarked on some sort of treatment and that they are ready for their child to receive help from which they may at times be excluded. This may help prevent them from sabotaging his therapy; they should also be kept informed of goals and progress in a general way so that they feel included as parents.

## CRISIS TREATMENT

When a major injury has put him in hospital, or when his abuse has been discovered and his family first comes into contact with an official agency, the child may be sharing the crisis with his parents. If he is still home, he may be having difficulty with the guilt he is feeling at somehow being responsible for the family's being 'in trouble'. He may be fearful of his parents' anger – and rightly so, for although they may no longer dare to punish him, they may also feel that he is to blame for their trouble and may tell him so. When follow-up appointments are made after an initial mild injury, we should arrange not only to check the child physically, but also to learn something of how he and the parents are reacting to the recent events. This may be the time to arrange for a psychological evaluation of the child, if it is suspected the child has suffered long-lasting psychological damage from the abuse.

The child hospitalized for a severe injury has to cope with pain as well as the knowledge that his parent can feel such violent anger towards him. The hospital is strange and frightening, and some of the procedures to which he must submit are likely to be painful. He is also separated from his parents and has to relate to many strange caregivers, usually without knowing what is going to happen next. Indeed, his parents may not be available to comfort him when he becomes a hospital patient. They themselves will be frightened and preoccupied with what is going to happen to them; sometimes they simply disappear without saying goodbye or reassuring their child that they will be back.

The hospital staff can do much to help the child immediately. They can recognize the pain, confusion, and fear he may not be able to voice or even show in his behaviour. They can reassure him, as much as possible, that his parents will be back. They can tell him, so far as they are able, what is going to happen to him in the hospital. They can assign him as few caregivers as possible, and they should include a special foster grandmother if they can.

If the child is to remain in the hospital for several days, his stay may be a useful opportunity for developmental and psychiatric evaluations. In any case, some time with a 'play lady' (a trained child specialist who can provide him with therapeutic play activities) or an interested nurse can give him an opportunity to express his feelings verbally or in play, and also to ask questions. For those children who are immobilized by casts, traction or burn dressings, some play (perhaps with puppets) that is vocally aggressive can help to relieve some of the tension he feels at being immobilized, and perhaps some of his anger at the violence done to him. How much children use such outlets depends on their personalities and their ages; younger children may wish only to be comforted, held and loved. If a child is to go directly to foster care from the hospital, his social worker should explain this to him carefully – perhaps together with his parents. The social worker, who will be keeping a close watch on his progress, will find it helpful to visit him in the hospital to tell him about his foster home and alert the people on the ward he knows best so that he can ask them questions. She can also ask them about his behaviour and his problems. The more she can see of him, the less he will feel deserted. She will also have to interpret his behaviour to the foster parents when he goes to them, and visit them frequently to prepare both them and the child for reinvolvement with the family.

## PHYSICAL CARE

Major injuries will need follow-up treatment, which can be long and complicated, as in the case of burns. Besides this medical treatment, it may be necessary to check whether the injuries have produced permanent consequences – for instance, whether head injuries have resulted in neurological damage. It will also be important to check for developmental delays. An occupational therapist will have suggestions to help those children whose large-muscle motor development has been held back by not being able to run and play like other children. Those children with delayed speech will improve to some extent as their social relationships improve and their contact with a responsive environment grows. But most of them will need speech therapy too.

## INDIVIDUAL PLAY THERAPY

Individual therapy would undoubtedly benefit every abused child. It is tragic that we can only bring this treatment to a small proportion of those in need because we know that *all* abused children, not only those referred, have difficulties that affect their school performance as well as their relationships with adults and other children. Some of them show signs of severe disturbance.

But the professional time needed, and therefore the expense, have thus far restricted individual play therapy to those few of the most disturbed children whose behaviour is particularly disruptive. These are mostly the hyperactive and aggressive children whose behaviour needs somehow to be contained before they can belong to any group or benefit from any other kind of treatment such as a play school. However, those children whose experiences have been particularly severe also receive individual therapy. Among such children are those who have seen their parent kill a brother or sister, or those who have been severely abused and then abandoned by one or other of their parents. Some of these children have become so disorganized and confused by their chaotic environments and experiences of violence that they can hardly distinguish reality from terrifying fantasy.

Children are not usually referred for psychiatric therapy as early as three or four, but some of our very disturbed children are as young as this and we believe they can be reached at least by a model treatment programme with limited goals. There are real difficulties in carrying on play therapy with children whose language is limited, unreliable and difficult to understand, but they are not insurmountable. This is because, first and foremost, providing a stable, reliable and understanding relationship does not depend primarily on words, but on consistent responses to a child's feelings so far as they can be understood through his behaviour. Gradually a therapist can come to understand the child's communications; for one thing, she can voice them and see if he confirms or denies them. Since many young abused children have such difficulty with language, play has to be the tool of communication, and it is remarkable how much of his daily-life story a child will reveal in dramatic play with dolls, puppets or animals. It may be a long time before he is ready to discuss his family life, but long before that the therapist can show that he understands and accepts the feelings the dolls are expressing, and that gives the child confidence that his feelings will be accepted too.

One little boy, whom we saw in play interviews while he was hospitalized for mild abuse, kept dropping on the floor first the mother doll and later the father and boy dolls as well, saying in a voice of desolation, 'Dead! Dead!' When we learned more of his family history, we came to the conclusion that he was reliving a period a year earlier when his mother had taken an overdose of drugs and had to go into hospital, and some later times when she and his new stepfather had fought, mostly about him. Although his behaviour on the ward was sometimes provocative, no one had realized he was still very worried or angered by these earlier events. Since, despite his limited verbal ability, he was able to express his distress in play, is was possible to investigate and treat it.

Another thirty-month-old boy with neurological difficulties, which included being very backward in talking, became severely frustrated when we were testing his speech development. He began crying and, in spite of our attempts to console him, lay weeping on the floor. After a couple of minutes he pulled down his shorts; for him the natural result of crying was a spanking and he was expected to co-operate!

A little four-year-old had been severely abused early in life by his mother. She had also kept him in a large cupboard as the only way she could separate herself from him in their small apartment. Eventually Timmy's mother deserted the family, and his father assumed both parental roles rather successfully. Because Timmy had difficulty communicating, not only because of his poor speech but because of his loose thought connections, we saw him in individual therapy. He had great difficulty believing that his therapist would be there at the appointed times, and when she told him that she would be going away on vacation, he reacted with a lot of play using planes and cars. In his play he controlled the separation by driving the cars and planes himself. Whenever Timmy became angry and felt alienated he retired to a cupboard; gradually he came to recognize and acknowledge this as repeating the early experience with his mother.

In individual play therapy, as in any form of therapy for abused children, the essential first goal is to build trust. This usually takes a good deal of time and a strenuous effort to remain as reliable as possible, giving the child plenty of warning of absences and other potential disappointments. As in all psychotherapy, vacations and changes in the timing of appointments are important, but an abused child needs even more help than most in expressing the sadness, betrayal and anger he feels. Although many of the older children (from five to eight) we see in treatment may give no open sign that their relationship to the therapist is important to them, they are always eager to come to therapy sessions, and their investment in treatment hours is clearly much greater than their limited acknowledgement of it. The children's difficulty in overcoming mistrust is often revealed in the way they readily accept disappointment as confirmation of the eventual disillusionment they constantly expect. They frequently misinterpret something done for their benefit as done for the convenience of their therapist. Sometimes the children are encouraged by their parents to mistrust their therapists. They may be made to feel that any problem they reveal will be used against their parents and might lead to separation. This can sometimes become a major stumbling block in treatment, since it puts the child in a real quandary as to what to believe. He may feel he must avoid talking about anything to his therapist. When this difficulty cannot be dealt with because the parents refuse to discuss it, the therapist can only try by his behaviour to show the child that he is trustworthy and to show the parents that he does not want to undermine the family ties.

The constant and central duty of the therapist is to maintain a firm picture of reality within the playroom, clear and available for contrast with the small patient's fantasy world and his experience in the outside world. This makes the inconsistencies of his home world clearer to the child and opens the way for new ways of behaving. One seven-year-old girl we saw had nearly been expelled from school because of her aggressive outbursts towards other children, and her inability to pay attention to her work. At home, she lived a life of confusion, occasional abuse and continuous neglect. Although boisterous and hyperactive outside the playroom, she insisted on the most rigid kind of school play during her treatment hours. Simultaneously, she began to be attentive at school and do good work. It seemed as if, by controlling and making very precise the rules of her play, she could impose on her relationship with her therapist the only kind of orderliness and reliability she had ever known – that of the schoolroom. The rigid rules made her less anxious that she might express her anger, even though they limited the scope of her expression. Eventually, with more treatment, it is hoped she will be able to find safety in expressing verbally her anger and underlying loneliness.


## AGGRESSIVE CHILDREN

The aggressive, 'hyperactive' children, who represent so many of the abused children we see, are often reacting with disorganized behaviour to what seems to be an overwhelming anxiety, bordering on panic. It is striking how often these children, after a very few hours of therapy, shed their hyperactivity at the door and can play comparatively normally. Those early therapy hours will have been concerned with setting limits as calmly as possible (a therapist may even, on occasion, hold a child who attacks or tries to run away) while the child came to realize that in this place no violent attack would take place and no rejection would follow his misbehaviour. In our experience there are very few physiologically hyperactive children (who can be calmed only by drugs such as methylphenidate). We find that after a while the children's aggressive and testing behaviour in therapy is replaced by underlying sadness, feelings of deprivation, and longing for love, which are so very much more difficult for them to face. These children have little faith in their capacity to inspire affection and approval, although they desire it as intensely as any other child does. Eventually, many children end up in the lap of the therapist, even sucking on a water-filled baby bottle. When this kind of regression occurs, we accept it and talk to the child about how he wishes his relationship with his parent could be like this. Later, when his longing for babying has lost its accompanying guilt and he is less afraid of rejection, he can more readily face his anger and disappointment and, with the help of the therapist, accept it to some extent as real and appropriate. It is important not to arouse expectations in the child which his parents are not going to be able or willing to fulfill. It is better to help the child accept his parents as they really are than to encourage him to ask for more than they wish to give. Since they are in treatment too, they may advance sufficiently fast to empathize with his needs, but if they do not, his demands may result in anger and abuse, or in their breaking off his therapy because it is 'spoiling' him. Most abused children are very sensitive to the nuances that distinguish therapy from ordinary life and are careful to adjust their behaviour accordingly. It is remarkable how they remain compliant or antisocial with their parents, while behaving quite differently and gradually more appropriately with their therapists. They are increasingly likely to extend their appropriate behaviour to other settings such as school. The behavioural change may take place without much verbal discussion, and a therapist is sometimes surprised to find a child who has never accepted the therapist's suggestions or interpretations showing definite improvement in his behaviour elsewhere.

## WITHDRAWN CHILDREN

Compliant, withdrawn children are seen in treatment less often unless they show obvious signs of severe disturbance. But when they are, they are apt to uncover the same feelings as the aggressive children, revealing their anger as they recognize the safety of the playroom, and then going on to express their underlying depression and deprivation. One little girl we saw in treatment between the ages of three and four was struggling with the need to be perfectly behaved at all times. She was always beautifully dressed, compulsively clean, and very restricted in her play; she insisted that she was always very 'good'. On a few occasions when she was unable to manage a toy to her satisfaction, she dissolved into tears, and at first could not be encouraged to try again. Water play turned out to be her path to expressing unacceptable wishes to be messy. Much later, she could curl up like a baby, and in a baby's voice demand to be given every toy in the playroom, while she lay sucking on a bottle. When she first brought the little girl for treatment, her mother said she must have something physiologically wrong with her because in her withdrawn moods she 'smelt strange'. These moods were probably depression triggered by her mother's periodic rejection.

A child whose parents have abused him severely, and who have then voluntarily relinquished their rights to him or lost them in court, feels extreme ambivalence and fear in what should be his most important relationship. Such a child may have great difficulty developing trust in another mother. A child who has had a brother or sister fatally injured by parents, perhaps in his presence, carries a burden not only for his own future, which he may believe depends entirely on his own good behaviour, but also of guilt that he escaped the fatal punishment and of knowledge that his parents' threats are not fantasy but real. Not only does he face these dread problems, but he has to come to terms with losing a brother or sister he may have loved – in a competitive way or not – and with the finality of death. Studies of children who have lost brothers or sisters through death in much less frightening ways show that they need a great deal of therapeutic assistance. The additional problems of children who have lost brothers or sisters through parental violence are only now being studied.

Young children coping with physical abuse, or neglect without abuse, may also be trying to come to terms with an environment that is totally chaotic. Relationships are often transitory; home is not in the same place for long; basic physical care such as providing meals depends on the whim of the moment; and parental acceptance or rejection is quite unpredictable. A child between one and four, who is trying to achieve some sense of the permanence in his life of the people he needs, and some sense of identity, may be unable to cope with such difficult conditions. We have seen children all of whose energy is consumed under such circumstances in trying to attain some grasp of reality and make some sense out of confusion, and whose own feelings of identity are very much jeopardized. Their problems are especially difficult if the parents' own identities are poorly defined – if they are inclined to reverse roles and act as children themselves. We have to help these children focus on reality and recognize distortions and inconsistencies.

## THERAPEUTIC PLAY SCHOOL

As we know, children who have been abused or severely neglected are poorly equipped to cope with an environment other than the one to which they have strenuously adapted all their lives. Among the characteristics needed for a healthy adjustment to school and to other children are a measure of independent identity, an ability to control one's behaviour, and an ability to communicate effectively. These are the very traits abused or neglected children have not been free to develop. What is more, it is unlikely that the abusive parents will have encouraged their intellectual development or fostered any sense of purposefulness.

A therapeutic play school or preschool can help to deal with these problems. It need not be elaborate, being distinguished by its philosophy rather than by its equipment. First it provides a sanctuary where for a given number of hours each week an abused child can develop total confidence in his safety and acceptance. It may take him months to come to trust the staff and the other children, but once he has, the rest of the programme can proceed more effectively. Trust is built up in many ways; it is based on firm routines that relieve the child of the strain of needing to predict what is going to happen next. The behaviour of the staff also needs to be predictable, and they must state clearly their expectations of each child and their reasons for those expectations. This explicitness helps a child understand how people about him think and allows him to behave with others in a clear and orderly way, perhaps for the first time in his life. In effect, it does for the child of three what an ideal mother would have done when he was a child of eighteen months; it interprets in words (thus making them part of his useful tools for living) the child's simple activities and interactions, helping him turn them into experience that can be understood. By this means children begin to feel that their behaviour will produce results they can count on, and that therefore they have some control over what happens to them. They also learn that what the staff members say and what they do are the same, and that he can count on them too.

Generally, before this predictability and trust can develop, a child in preschool needs to learn to express himself and to find his behaviour and speech accepted with understanding, if not approval. Many children arrive at school never having experienced the full attention of any adult as they expressed their own feelings. In school, a child finds his feelings taken seriously and given weight in a decision. Abused children often have not learned to express any feelings at all. They have learned to stifle even the most elementary expressions of pain on physical injury, and they need encouragement to express them in crying or in words. The simple statement, 'That must have hurt', when a child falls, may represent the first permission he has had to acknowledge pain. Likewise, his wishes for attention, affection, possession of a toy, or recognition of hunger or fatigue may all have been repressed, he may have assumed his needs were not worthy of recognition. To find his resentment or anger being recognized without immediate retaliation may be a new and, at first, a frightening experience; it is hard for some abused children to believe that their anger might be understood and even condoned. A school staff member may say, 'I think that might make me angry, too. Why don't you tell Johnny he can't have your truck until you've finished playing with it?' Thus, a child begins to realize that he too has rights and that the teacher will help him find a way to protect them. The staff also needs to help children who have learned only aggressive behaviour to distinguish between appropriate self-protection or justified anger and the bullying techniques they may have developed as the best way of getting along in a world where might is right. Much of this sounds like the ordinary learning to get along with other children required in any nursery school. However, it is only when one has observed the gradual emergence of intense emotion from a child who seemed stolid and compliant that one realizes how invisible, at first, an abused child's true feelings can be.

Most abused or neglected children are apt to relate first to one of the adults, who can actively help them feel safe in the school, rather than to another child. A new child may pick out the person with whom he feels most comfortable; whenever possible, this kind of overture is to be encouraged. Gradually his capacity to trust others increases, and he can be comfortable with most of the adults he sees every day. Some children find it much harder to be comfortable with other children, who share the same difficulty or who are seen as rivals for care and attention. Some abused children, however, have learned to band together with their brothers or sisters to comfort and care for one another; in the school setting these children may be very tender with a few of their playmates.

Thus, gradually and carefully, a foundation of trust and confidence can be laid down on which a child can develop a sense of his individuality and identity, with some self-respect and a sense of worth. These tasks must be at least partly accomplished before the child can adjust his behaviour reasonably to the day's events and before he is ready to explore the opportunities for learning that are part of toddler play and that prepare him for school experience.

We have to keep in mind that abused children are often seriously delayed developmentally, and that when we ask them questions or ask them to do things, their responses are likely to be distorted by anxiety about performing. For this reason, it is important to give them special experience in learning tasks, in such a way that the emotional impact of being asked a question or to perform a task is defused. When a child has had enough experience with doing small tasks and not being criticized or punished for failures; he will be more willing to keep on trying and will gradually come to see tasks as ends in themselves and not only means to approval and attention. For children who find them difficult, such tasks are best incorporated in the school programme very gradually, and only after the children have become secure enough to tolerate some failure. The tasks chosen must also be simple – suited to the children's levels of accomplishment, rather than to their chronological ages – for early success is important in building courage and confidence.

There may be other delays in development or missing aspects of experience that leave an abused or neglected child poorly prepared to make his way in a group, or even to use the simplest bodily skills. Unbelievably, many children have had no experience playing with toys or even in using their own bodies to play. The opportunity to run and jump and climb may be new, and they may need to overcome clumsiness and fearfulness before catching up. Parental disapproval of play as frivolous or messy may have constricted their ability to exploit toys and make it hard for them to feel free to enjoy toys and play. Seeing teachers playing on a childlike level, and enjoying it, may be a revelation that opens new opportunities for such children.

OTHER KINDS OF THERAPY IN DAY CARE OR SCHOOL

The same principles of caring for abused children can be applied to varying degrees in any nursery school or day-care centre. The advantage of ordinary nursery schools is that they offer the abused child daily contact with children who have not been abused and who can act as models of normal inter-action in the same way that the teachers can. What is needed in such a setting is one adult who can make herself specially available to the abused child so that he can begin to form a relationship and to interpret his new environment.

Some kind of individual help should also be made avail-able to the older schoolchild, when it is known that his parents are receiving help but that there is no programme of treatment for him. It is often possible for someone on the staff at school – a teacher, a social worker, a nurse – or some-one outside, say a priest or lay therapist, to offer such a child regular time in which he is free to talk, play, and develop the opportunity to trust and rely on someone. Such a relation-ship must not be treated lightly by the adult, and it should never be summarily closed off; the child should be allowed to take the initiative in ending it if he wishes. Big Brother and Big Sister programmes can provide this valuable service. Like all volunteer programmes they need to be well super-vised, so that the child's problems are adequately understood and there are safeguards against letting him down. The parents' support or co-operation is also needed.

## FOSTER CARE AND ITS ALTERNATIVES

Often the first step in planning any kind of care for an abused or severely neglected child is to remove him tempo-rarily from home. If his physical condition does not warrant hospitalization, even for diagnosis, it may seem appropriate to place him in temporary foster care until the whole family is diagnosed and a complete treatment plan organized. Foster care has the merit of keeping the child safe during a time of family crisis, although it does have some disadvantages as well. Perhaps the most subtle, but powerful, effect of immediate fostering is that relief from worry about his safety tempts everyone to allow the fostering to continue too long, and indeed to create a treatment plan based on long-term fostering. For the child this means separation from his family, which while it may relieve him of his fear of violence, also means the probably frightening loss of the only parents and the only kind of love he has known. Many abused children have totally accepted what is to them a fact of life – that love comes mixed with anger, criticism, demands, and punishment. They see separation as a true loss and feel rejected or even punished, for they assume that it is their own bad behaviour that is responsible for their having to be placed in foster care. For the parents, too, separation means punishment and the loss of a child they may have expected, though inappropriately, to meet their needs for love. Separation usually keeps alive their longing for the idea of the child but does not help them to revise or understand better the reality of their own child.

It would seem, therefore, that prolonged foster care should be avoided when possible, and every effort made to reunite parents and child, if only in a limited way, early in treatment. The exceptions, of course, would be those situations where the prognosis is so severe that parental rights are likely to be terminated because the child can probably never be safely returned.

One of the difficulties with fostering is that it is difficult for parents to see their child regularly, since the foster parents need to be protected from invasion and since visiting would be likely to disrupt the fostering relationship. Indeed, because the foster parents know only the child and are often appalled by the physical and emotional injuries he has suffered, they naturally often have the most indignant and critical feelings about his parents. Parents likewise harbour resentment against the foster parents, whom they see as taking away their child and presuming to offer him a better home than they can. Moreover, they expect the criticism and disapproval the foster parents probably feel. When the situation is potentially so explosive, it is small wonder that busy welfare departments usually do not try to bring child and parent together. In general, the parents do not see their child at least for the first ten days of his fostering, and thereafter see him only once (or rarely twice) a week for one or two hours in a room of the welfare department building. These visits are often distressing for everyone concerned. The child cries and begs to go home during early visits and then gradually begins to feel estranged and finds it hard to respond to his parents as he begins to make a relationship with his foster family. He then feels guilty, which complicates his already ambivalent feelings. The parents are very sensitive to their child's responses and feel helpless to counteract them, especially in the artificial circumstances of the welfare department. The welfare worker, who supervises and monitors the visit, also has ambivalent feelings – on the one hand looking for signs of difficulty in the relationship and, on the other, hoping for improvement. It is not easy for her to interpret the child's unhappiness. Is it due to the difficulties in the relationship with his parents or to his distress at separation from them? The parents' constraint and awkwardness in handling the child may result from the unnatural circumstances or their uneasiness at being close to him. The changes in the child in the course of fostering – as he becomes more expressive and active and shows obvious improvement in development – may be devastating to the parents, who recognize that their child is responding in the foster home as he could not in their own.

In order to avoid such deterioration in the parent-child relationship, some authorities have experimented with residential or day-care treatment for the whole family, rather than fostering. At the National Center in Denver, for example, families stay for a period of three to six months. The father is expected to continue his work while the mother and children spend all their time in the Center, with the child attending preschool if this seems to be indicated. There are three families in residence at any given time. Emphasis is always on the family as a unit, and treatment is offered to the parents separately, together, and in interaction with their children. A totally residential programme has some serious disadvantages – as we have seen. A modified version of this programme has the parents living at home, while the father works and maintains his household, but has both parents spending as much time as is feasible in a treatment centre where the child is living. This is less expensive and disruptive of family life. It means that the parents can undergo intensive treatment for their personal needs and marital problems, while at the same time learning how to handle their child better in daily sessions and through specific teaching and treatment. However, it does expose the child to a number of different caregivers when the parents are not there. Another programme uses specially selected foster homes where parents are welcomed from the very beginning, and in which the foster parents see their role as reuniting the parents and child rather than protecting and caring for the child alone.

Any treatment programme that attempts to help such severely handicapped people as these parents and their abused children must necessarily expect its ideal goal – to help the family attain full harmony – to be a very long way off and difficult to reach. All treatment is a clumsy effort to find solutions that are often beyond the budgets and personnel available. But it is also an effort to learn something about what works. It is hoped that the knowledge gained will be usable later in less expensive programmes.

## HOSPITALIZATION AND INSTITUTIONAL CARE

We have seen very few children who are autistic or schizophrenic in our work with abused children. Such children have usually been diagnosed as severely ill quite early on and have been sent to hospital or into intensive psychiatric care. It is true that occasionally schizophrenic and autistic children are abused, and, in a few of the cases we have seen, it seemed likely that the child's condition was a direct result of his very severely disturbed relationship with his mother. We still do not know exactly what the relation is, if there is one, between severe parental abuse or neglect and psychotic illness in children. We do know that some children who are made into family scapegoats become very disturbed and suffer from severe depression or anorexia nervosa as schoolchildren. This seems to be the result of absorbing as valid the distorted 'bad' picture of themselves that their family gives them.

## GROUP TREATMENT

Treatment of preadolescent or adolescent children in groups of four to eight has been used very effectively for all kinds of problems. But so far the group treatment of children specifically for abuse or neglect has been limited. Many of the children previously recommended for group treatment for other reasons are also victims of abuse or neglect. The results, though, are promising. At the National Center in Denver, one group of schoolchildren aged five to eleven, chosen because of their history of mild abuse and neglect, has now been meeting once a week for a year. With two therapists, one male and one female, they spend their time together in free or structured activity, eating snacks, and talking. It is impressive how much the ability of these emotionally handicapped children to relate to one another has grown. Their behaviour at school, which was previously very withdrawn or disruptive, has generally shown considerable improvement. Even though they had never been referred for treatment, these mildly abused children were in great need of help. Indeed, one girl needed residential treatment, so severe were her problems.

The co-operation of the parents of these children was in most cases minimal. The therapists or a staff member provided transportation, and the parents were rarely capable of more than passively allowing their children to attend the group. Similar groups are being tried with children subjected to sexual abuse.

Certainly the use of groups instead of individual psychotherapy seems a most promising approach, but until we understand better which methods work best and why, it may not offer a tremendous saving of time and personnel.

With each year of our experience, we believe more strongly in the importance of providing prompt treatment for the children as well as the parents. When the abuse or neglect has gone on for a long time, treating the parents is not enough. Of the treatments we can offer, we are not sure how adequate play school and group therapy are, and we are now engaged in evaluating them. What does seem clear is that we need to be able to make better diagnoses of the children's pathology, as well as their parents', so that we can treat the entirely family more effectively.

# 8/The Untreatable Family

Treatability is a relative term; in general, every member of an abusive family requires treatment. But the plain fact is that in some cases a child may never thrive in his own family, no matter how excellent the treatment provided for the parents and no matter how long it is continued. It is an unfortunate fact, though, that many helping professionals make it an article of faith that they can help 'anyone' and also that not to try is in some way a betrayal of the profession of social work, or nursing, or psychiatry. This may be especially true if the professional focuses only on the problems of his patient (parent) and does not accept the fact that optimism about eventual success exposes the children to danger and developmental crippling.

With child abuse the whole *family* is disturbed and not each needy member alone. Experience over the past twenty years has taught us that it is futile, and even disastrous, to return an abused child repeatedly to a family that exists in name only, that is not and never will be capable of providing a nurturing environment, and that may well destroy the child unless he is promptly and permanently removed. But is it possible to make such grave diagnostic assessments of families early in treatment? In general, it is not only possible, but essential — and often life-saving. Further, to stop incurable parents from destroying their child is an act of mercy not only to him but to them as well. This is one of those areas where society must look after the best interests of all concerned, through early intervention by the court as *parens patriae.*

As we explained in Chapter 6, we find after careful examination of parents, the abused child, and his nonabused brothers and sisters that in roughly 10 per cent of cases the child cannot safely be returned to his parents within a reasonable time. In those instances we seek judicial review of our recommendation that parental rights be terminated and the child freed for speedy adoption. Often the court requires several months of attempted treatment before coming to this most serious decision. Sometimes the facts are so obvious that no delay is needed.

We recommend early termination of parental rights, instead of a prolonged effort at treatment, when the parents are members of one of the four groups described in Chapter 6. Those groups were the cruel abusers who might torture their children slowly and repetitively; the psychotics whose children form part of their delusional systems or borderline psychotic patients not amenable to treatment; the aggressive sociopaths who might unpredictably and lethally strike out when angered; and the fanatics, outwardly reasonable, respectable people with an encapsulated psychosis that could kill their children (such as a couple who believed their baby should live only on carrot juice, since all other food was poisonous).

Aside from the parents in these groups, there are others to whom we cannot recommend returning children who have had to be hospitalized. First are the parents so addicted to alcohol or drugs that they cannot provide even minimal care for their babies, not because they do not love them but because they are emotionally and intellectually unavailable to them. They cannot form the relationship upon which their children depend for normal development. And in the absence of proper care the risk of serious accidents mounts steadily.

Second are the families when the parents are too retarded or the mothers simply too young to raise children. This is a complicated evaluation: there is no single age or level of IQ which can be used as a boundary, since a great deal depends on what other caregivers there might be within the family.

But, in general, parents with IQs under sixty and mothers under fifteen years old seem to warrant a judicial review to determine whether termination of parental rights is indeed required.

Third are the families where other children have already been seriously injured, and where there may have been one or more unexplained deaths. With these families, we evaluate the high-risk factors according to the sort of checklist described in Chapter 5. We may then well recommend termination of parental rights.

These groups, seven in all, represent about ten per cent of the families with hospitalized abused children. They are found too, of course, among the families of children brought to the attention of child-protection services by schools, relatives, police, and neighbours. But since these children include many comparatively mild cases not requiring medical attention, the proportion of untreatable families in this category is much smaller.

We also seek termination of parental rights for the 10 per cent of abused children whose families, after six or nine months of treatment, show little or no improvement. There is another group of parents, unable to accept any kind of help within a reasonable time framework of six months to a year, who remain adamant about their right to treat their children as they see fit or who continue a lifestyle so chaotic and lacking in fixed relationships that they have little to offer their children. Although they do not fit into the usual defined categories of pathology with grave prognosis, their resistance to help, even when treatment is court-ordered, makes the prognosis hopeless. Also, we often seek termination successfully in cases of abandonment where an earnest effort has been made to locate the parents and they, in turn, have failed to communicate with their child or his caregiver for more than six months (or, in some jurisdictions, a full year).

We should stress that, when we say that a *family* is untreatable, we do not mean that the parents do not deserve treatment. What we mean is that the child should not be used as the instrument of treatment. Quite commonly, a professional who is treating a parent and who has overidentified with the needs of his patient will say that losing custody of the child will harm the parent and will set back his progress in treatment. But we firmly believe that a child's rights must be independently recognized. A child's developmental timetable simply does not allow undue delay. A parent may require three or four years of treatment before he can safely look after a child, but the child cannot wait that long in 'temporary placement'. There must be a more civilized way of dealing with incurable failures than providing a martyred child. Once an experienced social worker, psychiatrist and paediatrician have examined all the members of the child's family, we should have enough information to advise a court on whether a child will or will not be able to live safely in that family, either in the present or in the foreseeable future. It may seem intrusive and authoritarian to do this, but the fact is that in some cases there is no other safeguard for the child's health, normal development, or even life.

Clearly it is far better if the question of compulsory termination of parental rights never arises because the parents are prepared to relinquish voluntarily a child they can admit they do not want, and perhaps even hate. Interestingly, it is often family pressure that makes it hard for parents to agree to this, though they may express relief when involuntary termination then takes the matter out of their hands. We say 'The most loving thing you can do for this child and for yourself is to give both of you a new start,' or 'We really will not feel safe letting you have Jody back, so would you consider letting her have a new home?' In time, civilized society will come to accept voluntary relinquishment as socially acceptable, just as it has accepted divorce for incompatible couples.

# 9/What Future Do Abusive Families Face?

Once an abusive family has come to the attention of a child-protection service, the outcome for parents and children will depend on how disturbed the family is, how old the child is, how long he has been abused, and how it has affected him. The range of physical and emotional abuse is immense, and home conditions vary infinitely from family to family. Children also vary enormously in their responses to physical and emotional abuse or rejection by their parents. There are some children so strong and resilient emotionally that, though scarred, they can accept and benefit from whatever love and empathy comes their way from any adult or child; these children can tolerate behaviour that would totally disable a more vulnerable child. Virtually nothing is known about what lies behind these enormous differences in children's responses to their home conditions.

The children from the 80 per cent of abusive families we treat return home, either directly from the hospital or following a period in foster care. These children, in our experience, have *never* been injured again once we have been able to confirm four objective changes. First, the abusive parent's image of himself must have improved to the point where he has made at least one friend with whom he shares regular and enjoyable experiences, such as bowling. Second, both parents must have found something attractive in their abused child and be able to show it by talking lovingly, hugging, or cuddling. Third, both parents must have learned to use lifelines in moments of crisis, so that they telephone their social worker, a friend, or another member of Parents Anonymous, or else take their children to a crisis nursery. Last, weekend reunions with their child in hospital or foster care must become more and more enjoyable, and increasing responsibility must not have strained family life unduly. It is premature to return the child if these criteria have not been met; he will be attacked again, and probably much more severely. Of course, it is very important to be sure that the reason for the family's improvement is not the absence of the child because, if so, his return will obviously reverse the process.

Even after these minimal conditions have been met, some families will need years of support. But, provided they also are treated until they are much older, their children may be better off with them than in constantly changing foster homes. The problems that have to be considered in deciding whether they will be better off at home are, on the one hand, whether their parents' progress is really too slow for the children's developmental pace and, on the other, whether the ending of physical abuse is accompanied by any decrease in emotional abuse. This more insidious problem is only just coming to be recognized as a circumstance that requires intervention even in the absence of physical abuse, although without injury or noticeable failure to thrive, it may continue unrecognized. It is in the area of emotional abuse that most progress can now be expected.

Our long-term follow-up of abusive parents 'successfully' treated shows that there is no serious reinjury. But only in about half these families is there any change in the parents' basic feeling for their child, their capacity to be truly loving – in short, their 'character'. One mother said, 'I don't beat Johnny any more, but I hate the son-of-a-bitch like I always did.' Happily, most parents can understand and enjoy their child more. Their lives are improved by successful crisis management. And there is an added bonus: a frequent sign of a family's improved emotional health is that sexual satisfaction between the parents increases greatly; indeed, sometimes they attain sexual happiness for the first time.

Naturally, one must be realistic in assessing family treatment. Improvement is not likely to be swift, and this can be disappointing. But a mother and father who have themselves had an emotionally stunting start in life, have lived for twenty or thirty years in sterile or chaotic circumstances, and who have experienced the threat of losing their child, require years of loving and supportive contact while they gradually develop trust and the capacity to love. What is remarkable is that as many as 40 per cent of parents *do* grow and develop, usually through prolonged contact with one or two reliable and uncritical adults who provide the mothering and fathering they have never known. If these parents can stop their abuse, live less chaotic lives, manage better to support each other and nurture their children at least to some degree, then they show splendid progress. They have, indeed, come a long way.

The remaining 40 per cent, who can stop physically, but not emotionally, abusing their children at home are in many ways the least well served of all the families. Long-term care for such families is hard to find, and the situation of the abused child (and often of his nonabused siblings too) requires a really massive effort at improvement, for instance in the form of guaranteed therapeutic day care. The parents often do best in a Parents Anonymous group; by helping others they help themselves and enlarge their social spheres. Extra parenting from other loving adults is absolutely essential for the children, though it is currently the most neglected aspect of long-term family care. Overall results are best when therapy is oriented towards the family as a whole rather than just towards the parent actually performing the abuse. When dismal failure occurs, it is usually in the absence of family therapy. The parents' progress is always slow, whatever the circumstances, but the children's, if they are treated early, is often remarkably swift and profound.

FOLLOWING FORMER PATIENTS

We are in the midst of a follow-up study of the parents we

have treated, checking on them ten years and twenty years after our initial contact. It is already clear that our results conform to a pattern that is now familiar. The untreatable families could generally have been identified at once; children not rescued from them risked permanent brain damage or death. These families accounted for the standard 10 per cent of our sample. Then there were the treatment failures, who might not kill their children but who could develop no ties of affection at all. These accounted for another 10 per cent. Of the remaining 80 per cent, half required long-term support but are happier as families and can be considered safe and improving slowly; and the other half required only short-term help, became independent within one to three years, and are now not so different from a sample taken from the population at large.

All the disasters we experienced took place in situations where optimism about the successful progress of therapy was allowed to overrule the evidence. There were few real surprises. Most of the children who died did so while under the care of the court or a child-protection agency. The return of these children to their homes was decided on the basis not of proper assessments but of extraneous circumstances, and major crises that followed were ignored.

Ten per cent of our families have divorced or separated (a smaller proportion than in the population at large). Most of the families are finding life greatly improved; as children mature so do their parents, and it is striking how many recall the helpful people (often a male therapist and a female therapist) who turned things around for them. Our sample of families was drawn from all social classes, and, interestingly, no class differences are revealed by the follow-up study: families from all socioeconomic levels have improved equally.

When we turn to look at the long-term effects of abuse on the children, we find ourselves with a problem of method. To isolate the effects of abuse itself, we need to compare the abused children with others whose experience has been similar in every other important respect. But we cannot simply compare abused children with their nonabused brothers and sisters, because the latter may have been quite as deprived emotionally and indeed may be far more ill. Studies commonly focus on children who have suffered 'true' accidents; but the fact is that chaotic, disaster-prone homes may show accident rates twenty times higher than average homes, and in terms of IQ or emotional environment the children from those places may have much in common with our abused group. Using 'other hospital admissions' for comparison is likewise unreliable because in any given case the doctor may have decided for social as much as for medical reasons to treat the child in the hospital rather than at home.

In looking at long-term effects we also have to sort out the influence of our well-meaning, life-saving interventions, which in some cases could constitute unintentional abuse. Following up nearly sixty abused children from Denver, five years after treatment, associates of ours found that a third of them had changed homes three to *eight* times in an average of four and a half years. Consider one little six-year-old girl who at twelve months had suffered a skull fracture and a leg fracture along with other injuries inflicted by her mother. She would have been killed if returned home, but instead of terminating parental rights our justice system put her through thirteen homes in five years, including one where adoption was unsuccessfully attempted. She is only mildly handicapped by her injuries, but emotionally rather severely handicapped by the years that passed before she became available for adoption. At six she is a bright child but finds learning difficult, cannot become attached to any one person, and acts out her disturbance. All in all, she is an unhappy little girl whose future holds a continuous series of unsuccessful foster-home placements. Our poor management has crippled this child far more than her skull and leg fractures.

The classic follow-up study of abused children was published by Elizabeth Elmer and G. S. Gregg in 1967.[1] They looked at 52 cases, of whom 12 were either dead or in institutions for the retarded (it is not clear why they chose to combine these two groups). Of 33 children they evaluated in detail, an appalling 88 per cent were judged as damaged; they were mentally retarded or showed significant emotional disorders, speech defects, or marked physical handicaps. Elmer has recently published another study comparing 17 abused children eight years after abuse with another group of children hurt in accidents thought to be genuinely accidental. She found school performance and social adjustment equally poor for both groups but since, as we know, their backgrounds may have been equally violent, chaotic, and neglectful, that is perhaps not very surprising.

A. Sandgrun has managed to point out clear differences between three groups of children: abused, neglected, and mildly disadvantaged economically.[2] Especially striking are the results of Harold Martin and his associates in our Colorado group.[3] They looked at 58 children five years after treatment – children, incidentally, far less severely abused than is usual for child-abuse studies – and found some neurological abnormality in all but five of them. Eighteen of the children showed abnormalities severe enough to handicap them in their everyday lives. But it was only the severe damage that could be explained by obvious brain injury. Nearly half the children who showed no sign of head injury nonetheless showed signs of neurological damage (though we should remember of course that severe shaking can damage the brain without any detectable mark on the head). Importantly, children abused while already failing to thrive were likelier to be impaired than those abused while well nourished.

Looking at studies of neurological impairment generally, we find that 20 to 50 per cent of abused children are significantly damaged. This is discouraging, but against it we can set the fact that most of the children studied have remained in unsatisfactory environments and have not received the treatment described in Chapter 7. We find that, given appropriate intervention and family therapy from the start, much better results are possible.

The children in our own therapeutic nursery school and the school-age children in Martin's study lag behind normal children in two main ways: in language development and in physical skills beginning with crawling and walking. They are consistently better, though, at delicate movements, adapting to new situations, and relating to other people. Interestingly, even the children without neurological defects still show the same developmental lag. It is unlikely that lack of stimulation alone can account for these striking findings. It is far more probable that talking as well as jumping, skipping, running, and other lively behaviour are so strongly discouraged in the abusive home, where the child's needs come way behind the parents', that the child can never develop these skills for fear of trouble and injury. These children do not learn to communicate and tend to have school problems as a direct result. Indeed, as noted earlier in the book, a child may fantasize that he is not even seen if he can avoid eye contact.

When we are dealing with preschool abused children, we use three tests to see how they are improving. None of these is found in standard psychology texts. First, we use the eye-contact test; as a child grows less fearful and more trusting he establishes and eventually comes to enjoy eye contact. Second, we have the lap test; we note when a child first learns that a lap is a safe haven and returns whenever he needs reassurance during a nursery session. Ultimately, he comes to need only a hug. Last, we use the sweet test; offered a bowl of sweets a new child will take lots if he dares to take any. He crams them into every pocket and fills both hands as well. As he improves, he takes fewer until he gets down to two. (We have not yet got anyone down to one.)

As we have future opportunities for follow-up studies of the patients seen at the Center, we expect to learn even more about the various prospects of children living in once-abusive families. We need to proceed cautiously in drawing conclusions from the findings of children who do go home; nevertheless, these findings tend to verify the Center's guidelines in determining which children should return home and, as a result, add to our cautious optimism about the futures of those who do.

# 10/A Comprehensive, Community-Wide Approach

Child abuse, even if we exclude emotional deprivation, is a very widespread problem, and the consciousness is growing that traditional child-protection agencies are simply not equal to it. It is no criticism of them to say that they have neither the funds nor the staff to make the necessary impact. Nor can they possibly bring to bear all the skills this multi-faceted problem requires. What is needed, and what is now beginning to be created, is a new and more broadly based approach that will draw more effectively on the resources of the community.

It is frequently better to plan and implement a community-wide programme from scratch than to try to change the existing agencies, which may be defensive about their short-comings, convinced that additional money would solve all their problems, and jealous of their traditional roles. Many American communities have found it necessary to take a fresh look at the problem from the citizen's point of view. Task forces or councils have been formed, often spear-headed by prominent members of the community or a few concerned professionals. Out of these efforts have come truly exciting comprehensive programmes that have broad community and often legislative support. In some areas the official child-protection services have recognized, that in order to get community support, they had to make their closed system an open one, and they have themselves initiated citizen councils on child abuse.

What are the basic ingredients of a community-wide plan? First, there must be recognition that putting the whole burden of responsibility on the social worker will no longer work and that a broadly based team effort – using experts from many disciplines – should take the place of that system. In this kind of system social workers are the leaders, assisted, as equal and valued partners, by a team of additional professionals, including a paediatrician, a health visitor, a representative of the police, a lawyer, a psychologist or psychiatrist, and, if at all possible, a member of the lay public as well. In the past, social workers who were looking after potentially abusive families were forced, ludicrous though it seems, to reach beyond their skills in casework, into the medical, legal, psychiatric, and law-enforcement fields, without either training or back-up. Quite apart from being ineffective, this system is immensely stressful. It is no surprise to find a recent review of the existing 3300 county child-protection departments in America indicating a really alarming rate of staff turnover: 50 to 100 per cent of primary caseworkers in child protection leave each year, many ostensibly in pursuit of a higher academic degree but, more truthfully, because the emotional and physical strains have become too much for them to bear.

There are ways we can lighten the load of social workers and make them more effective. The problem of professional 'burn out' could be faced and job turnover reduced to, say, 15 per cent by allowing every social worker a period during which no new cases were assigned. During these periods, which should total at least two or three weeks every three months, the hard-pressed worker should be able to evaluate his current cases and those in foster care, train newer workers, and improve his contact with the schools in his area.

Constant contact with other professionals on the team would make social workers better able to share decision making. And the emotional support, encouragement, and broadened intellectual experience those professionals can give should, in combination with workers' own personal qualities of optimism and humour in the face of grim realities, dramatically reduce staff turnover and increase job satisfaction and effectiveness.

Social workers also clearly need to be given far more professional freedom and scope for creativity by their supervisors. As a profession, social work has long tended to treat its own members as dependent children – to a degree unmatched in any other way of life. Clearly, a beginning worker needs supervision, perhaps for a year, but then consultation should take its place; and in token of this the term 'supervisor' should give way to 'team leader'. It follows, of course, that team leaders have to remain professionally competent by keeping clients of their own; that has the advantage of ensuring they never forget how emotionally draining dealing with child abuse can be.

All those involved in building a community-wide plan need a clear understanding of three distinct phases in the management of child abuse: first, crisis management, which includes diagnosing the family situation and developing a long-term treatment plan for each family member; second, carrying out those plans (as described in Chapters 6 and 7); and third, raising the consciousness of other professionals and the community, evaluating the work done, and researching further into the problem and its remedies.

It is the lot of child-protection departments to focus on crisis management in emergencies. Many workers would like to give long-term treatment to parents and even begin to assess and treat children, but their caseloads are so large that they are overwhelmed by the sheer number of children whose cases need investigating and evaluating. Many social workers in the United States can spend only two hours a month with a mother, have even less time for the father, and none at all for the child. Often, three to six months is the time limit set for even this inadequate care. Obviously, the minimum effective treatment time is much greater than this; we believe that five hours a month – sixty hours a year – for each family is the least that is acceptable. Clearly, no single worker can be giving that sort of time to more than twenty-two families at any one point. Yet many in fact handle well over a hundred. Compare this to the long-term care that can be given by parent aides, lay therapists who work with carefully selected families in close collaboration with a social worker or psychiatrist and who can regularly spent twenty to fifty hours a month with a family.

Although an official child-protection service has a role to play in long-term care, its primary concern currently is with prompt and efficient crisis care, family evaluation, and the development of treatment plans. No one social worker can manage crisis care, long-term care, education, research, and evaluation all at the same time, though it might be desirable for her to alternate between them. Long-term therapy has to be shared with outsiders. Often the community council can find potential contributors to treatment in the community, among them former adoption agencies, church groups, and orphanages that, with proper encouragement and some financial support, will supplement long-term care for adults and children. Links between public and private agencies and the development of needed new services can often be better organized by community councils than by any one group. Few agencies like to be assigned tasks, but most want to be regarded as performing an important role in the community.

The third aspect of building a community-wide plan for preventing and treating abuse is education for professionals and the public. It requires that personnel be freed, for a time, from the constant pressure of families in crisis, as in the free period described above. Workers in child protection need to evaluate their performance constantly and routinely. Instead of scapegoats for particular failures, everyone should ask, 'How could we have done better and how will we change because of this experience?' Since major decisions are jointly made, no one person is ever solely responsible, *all* are responsible, for good decisions and bad. Human conduct is hard to predict, and it makes sense to share life-and-death decisions across professional lines so that if a child is reinjured or killed after being prematurely returned to his parents it is possible to say whether the wrong recommendation was avoidable or not. Similarly, when courts ignore the recommendation of a child-protection team and disaster follows, they should certainly know the outcome, though at present they are not routinely informed, at least in the United States. We learn from success and failure, and both should be out in the open. Instead of burying our mistakes, on the grounds for instance of 'client confidentiality' we should be aware that we are too often concerned with professional confidentiality; far better to say, 'We were wrong because . . .'

Building mutual trust in a team takes time and leadership, backed by community pressure. It does not simply depend on new funding, or on destroying existing institutions, though some may need a change in leadership if they are unwilling to share and co-operate in broadening and improving services.

Aside from the constant shortage of time and the maze of red tape, nothing is more frustrating to child-protection workers than the primitive nature of the services aimed at prevention. Always to be there *after* the event is clearly not good enough. Many workers are now beginning to get purposefully involved with maternity hospitals and in early child care so that they can help when abuse is likely but has not yet occurred.

Educating schoolchildren for family life has a place in preventing child abuse, at least in the case of young parents, who are almost totally unprepared for parenthood. But it would be naïve to think that great knowledge is the solution to the problem on its own. We know that even the most unskilled and youngest of mothers often succeed blissfully while the best educated and most intellectual sometimes do not. Sheer factual knowledge and skills are helpful for any parent, but to our best knowledge, having oneself had loving parents and having a supportive spouse remain the best guards against child abuse.

The media have their role to play in community planning and, increasingly, both the media and the community want public servants to be publicly accountable. Accurate, continuous reporting and monitoring of child-abuse programmes in the community is a valid function for press and television and should be encouraged by openness from social workers about the strengths and weaknesses of the system. Enlisting the help of the media to change laws or financial allocations, and to tell the public that families involved in child abuse *can* be rehabilitated, will help the community to be more concerned about its children.

# 11/Vindicating
## the Rights
## of Children

In 1792, Mary Wollstonecraft wrote tracts to vindicate the rights of women. Now, nearly two hundred years later, we need to vindicate the rights of children.

Our children, like our natural resources, are neither plentiful nor expendable. Most people would agree that children are entitled to a safe home in which to develop fully their inherent capacities. In a free society the difficult question is to decide the precise point at which the state should intervene when parents seem not to be providing this. The parents' right to raise the children as they see fit and the right to privacy without state intrusion must be balanced against a child's right to receive 'reasonable care and protection' and escape 'cruel and unusual punishment', as the law puts it. A distinguished American judge, criticizing a clause in the child-protection laws of his state which exclude refusal on religious grounds of medical treatment for a sick child, said, 'Children are citizens. Their right for life supersedes their parents' right to believe.'

'A man's home is his castle' is an idea most of us treat with respect. Certainly the police do, when they consider whether to intervene in a domestic quarrel (and understandably, since intervention in wife battering is the most frequent source of police injury). Unless the wife files a complaint, or there are repeated complaints from the neighbours, police tend to try to stay out of family matters. This is changing, however, particularly where abused and neglected children are concerned.

In Great Britain the fact that local health visitors and social workers have recently joined forces should improve the co-ordination of services between health professionals, social workers, and police. Other statutory agencies, such as the NSPCC in Britain, are similarly broadening their services and using professionals from different disciplines in an effort to reduce rivalry between agencies and improve the protection they offer. In Britain, until recently, it was impossible legally to terminate parental rights against the parents' wishes and to make the children available for adoption. As a result abused children faced foster care until they were grown up. Many courts in the United Kingdom have only just begun to believe that child abuse truly exists. But many judges in Great Britain still demand the sorts of proof they would demand in a criminal case, even in a civil case involving simply taking a child into care. For centuries the child has been a chattel in common law, and still today for many judges the rights of children are not yet nearly so important as the rights of parents.

It is a disturbing fact that virtually only working-class families are dealt with by the courts and social services. Middle-class families abusing their children are handled by doctors who, even if they can assure the safety of the child, may not be able or willing to cope with the family's emotional needs. In most instances, neighbours tend to 'mind their own business' and are reluctant to get involved in other people's lives.

Child abuse is less common in families who have other relations living with them. Children in these 'extended' families can count on a number of loving adults for protection and care. If families could come to lead less isolated lives in the community, so that the arrival of a new baby in the neighbourhood were again a reason for community celebration and the parents could turn for support to a larger circle of neighbours and friends, then children's well-being would be far better assured. Each child would be truly everybody's child.

One radical but effective move to improve children's

safety would be to make them full citizens, entitled to all rights except the vote. This would mean that parents could not refuse their children basic health services. A baby's weight gain, basic immunizations, early checks for and correction of birth defects, and child guidance where needed would not be left to the discretion of the parents. If obstetricians, paediatricians, nurses, and health visitors had to make routine observations during pregnancy and after birth, prevention of serious child abuse could start where it should. But for this to happen, society has to agree that intervention is not 'for' the child and 'against' the parents, as people seem to feel now, but is *for the family*. Health visitors, in particular, could do a great deal if they broadened their role as instructors in the skills of child care to include assessing and encouraging parents' performance in nurturing the child physically and emotionally. It is not lack of skill that stops health professionals from offering such guidance (giving up makes them feel guilty and unprofessional), but timidity, confusion over their 'rights', and inadequate back-up by the local authorities and courts. They, along with many social workers, often cannot face the fact that some parents simply are not able to act as parents.

If doctors and social service departments intervened early, families that are treatable could get the help they so badly need before the child is badly damaged. In untreatable families early termination of parental rights would free the child for prompt adoption. Abuse has such a profound and scarring effect on a child's personal development and educational success that he, and often his brothers and sisters too, must be treated as soon as the abuse is discovered. Long-term foster care, if the child is shifted from one home to another, creates so many additional harmful problems that it must be used with great caution.

Many countries have been moving towards increasing the protection they provide for children. In Holland, for example, where doctors are as reluctant to report child abuse as they are anywhere else, a simple approach has largely solved the problem. The doctor reports suspected child abuse to his district *Vertrauensartz* (confidential doctor), who is part of a multidisciplinary team including a social worker and co-ordinator. Because the family doctor is communicating his problem to another doctor, he feels less inhibited about it.

This policy is certainly getting help to children earlier. A variety of innovative treatment programmes, like the family residential units at the Park Hospital in Oxford, the Triangle in Amsterdam, and Circle House in Denver, are being developed all over the world. An interdisciplinary, international journal and biannual international meetings bring together workers on child abuse from all fields and many countries to exchange information and to lobby for further recognition of children's rights.

Although further research is urgently needed, enough is known now to enable us to move rapidly ahead in prevention, early diagnosis, and different kinds of treatment for adults and children. What is needed most of all is firm, early decision making for the greatest good of the child.

Although the cases reported in this book are distressing and horrifying, the situation for children is better now than at any time in history. Anyone who reads about physically or emotionally abused children, or deals with them daily, must sometimes feel pessimistic about whether we will ever be able to give every child the start in life he deserves. But it is important not to underestimate the huge strides now being made. We must not be demoralized or fail to keep pushing forward. Ultimately our children's future and our world's future are one.

# References

**1 THE DIMENSIONS OF THE PROBLEM**

1. For a good summary see S. X. Radbill, 'A History of Child Abuse and Infanticide.' In R. E. Helfer and C. H. Kempe, eds., *The Battered Child* (Chicago: University of Chicago Press, 1968).
2. A. Tardieu, *Etude médico-légale sur l'infanticide* (Paris, 1868).
3. A. A. W. Johnson, *Lectures on the Surgery of Childhood* (London, 1868).
4. J. Caffey, 'Multiple Fractures in the Long Bones of Children Suffering from Chronic Subdural Hematoma,' *American Journal of Roentgenology*, 1946, *56*, 163.
5. F. N. Silverman, 'The Roentgen Manifestations of Unrecognized Skeletal Trauma in Infants,' *American Journal of Roentgenology, Radium Therapy Nuclear Medicine*, 1953, *69*, 413.
6. P. V. Woolley and W. A. Evans, 'Significance of Skeletal Lesions in Infants Resembling Those of Traumatic Origin,' *Journal of the American Medical Association*, 1955, *158*, 539.
7. C. H. Kempe, *et al.*, 'The Battered Child Syndrome,' *Journal of the American Medical Association*, 1962, *181*, 17.
8. D. Gil, *Violence Against Children: Physical Abuse in the United States* (Cambridge: Harvard University Press, 1973), p. 138. See also D. Gil, 'Unraveling Child Abuse,' *American Journal of Orthopsychiatry*, 1975, *45*, 346.

**2 THE ABUSIVE PARENT**

1. K. Tennes, 'Personality Development of a Battered Child' (paper presented at Reiss Davis Child Study Center, Los Angeles, 1973).

3   THE ABUSED CHILD

1.  M. A. Lynch, 'Ill Health and Child Abuse,' *Lancet*, 1975, 2, 317-319.
2.  T. B. Brazelton, *Infants and Mothers: Differences in Development* (New York: Delacorte Press, 1969).
3.  S. Chess, A. Thomas, and H. O. Birch, 'Behaviour Problems Revisited: Findings of an Anterospective Study,' *Child Psychiatry*, 1967, 6, 321-331.
4.  T. B. Brazelton, *et al.*, 'The Origins of Reciprocity and the Early Mother-Infant Interaction.' In M. Lewis and A. Rosenblum, eds., *The Effects of the Infant on its Caregiver* (New York: Wiley, 1974).
5.  E. Tronick, *et al.*, 'Infant Emotions in Normal and Perturbated Interactions' (paper presented at meeting of Society for Research in Child Development, Denver, Colorado, April 11, 1975).
6.  E. H. Erikson, *Childhood and Society* (New York: Norton, 1963).
7.  B. Steele, 'Violence Within the Family.' In R. E. Helfer and C. H. Kempe, eds., *Child Abuse and Neglect: The Family and the Community* (Cambridge: Ballinger, 1976).


4   INCEST AND OTHER FORMS OF SEXUAL ABUSE

1.  H. Giarretto, *Humanistic Treatment of Father-Daughter Incest, Child Abuse and Neglect* (New York: Pergamon Press, 1977), I, 411-426.
2.  M. Mead, 'Incest.' In *International Encyclopedia of the Social Sciences* (New York: Crowell Collier and Macmillan, 1968).


6   TREATING ABUSIVE PARENTS

1.  M. Jeffrey, 'Practical Ways to Change Parent-Child Interaction in Families of Children at Risk.' In R. E. Helfer and C. H. Kempe, eds., *Child Abuse and Neglect: The Family and the Community* (Cambridge: Ballinger, 1976).

9   WHAT FUTURE DO ABUSIVE FAMILIES FACE?

1.  E. Elmer and G. S. Gregg, 'Developmental Characteristics of Abused Children,' *Pediatrics*, 1967, *40*, 596.
2.  A. Sandgrun, R. W. Gaines, and A. H. Green, 'Child Abuse and Mental Retardation: A Problem of Cause and Effect,' *Journal of Mental Deficiency*, 1975, *19* (no. 3), 327.
3.  H. Martin, *et al.*, 'The Development of Abused Children,' *Advances in Pediatrics*, 1974, *21*, 25.

# Suggested
# further reading

J. M. CAMERON, L. J. RAE, *Atlas of the Battered Child Syndrome* (New York, Churchill Livingstone, 1975). The best visual and radiologic atlas of physical abuse. This work is definitive.

JAN CARTER, ED., *The Maltreated Child* (Priory Press, 1974). The first integrated Interdisciplinary British contribution edited by a perceptive and innovative social worker. The volume clearly points up some of the difficulties in inter-disciplinary efforts of problems involved in helping the maltreated child.

N. B. EBELING, D. A. HILL, *Child Abuse: Intervention and Treatment* (Science Group Inc., 1975). This volume gives an excellent description of a working child protective system in Boston, Massachusetts, and is based on a conference sponsored by the Massachusetts Society for the Prevention of Cruelty to Children.

ELIZABETH ELMER, *Children in Jeopardy*, 4th ed. (Pittsburgh, University of Pittsburgh Press, 1977). This classic volume is a culmination of thirty years of effort in child protection based on extensive clinical and research experience by the Pittsburgh group.

V. J. FONTANA, D. J. BESHAROV, *The Maltreated Child: The Maltreated Syndrome in Children. A Medical, Legal and Social Guide*, 3rd ed. (Springfield, Ill., Charles C. Thomas, 1977). Comprehensive overview with excellent clinical vignettes, which can appeal to the professional and to the educated general public concerned about improving the lot of abused and neglected children by one of the pioneers in the efforts to improve treatment for abused and neglected children in New York. An excellent legal framework for child protection and model child protection act are features of this important third edition.

A. W. FRANKLIN, ED., *Concerning Child Abuse* (London and New York, Churchill Livingstone, 1975). A carefully edited monograph reporting on the first meeting of an interdisciplinary working group on child abuse held at Tunbridge Wells which attempts to bring about better co-ordination between helping services in the U.K.

A. W. FRANKLIN, ED., *Child Abuse: Prediction, Prevention and Follow-Up* (Edinburgh, London and New York, Churchill Livingstone, 1977). Report of the second meeting of the Tunbridge Wells working group on child abuse, again edited by the paediatrician who chairs the group and addresses the current state of knowledge of all issues involving prediction and prevention and follow-up to 1976, though not including most recent U.S. experience in prediction and prevention.

A. W. FRANKLIN, ED., *The Challenge of Child Abuse* (London and Grune and Stratton, New York, The Academic Press, 1977). A third book in the above series, again with a variety of excellent contributions in the broad field.

R. E. HELFER, C. H. KEMPE, EDS., *The Battered Child*, 2nd ed., (Chicago, University of Chicago Press, 1974). The first interdisciplinary presentation of the paediatric, radiological, pathologic, psychiatric, social work and legal description of physical abuse. Many of the concepts presented in the first edition are now incorporated as commonplace in protective services practice. The second edition is an update on U.S. laws, state by state.

R. E. HELFER, C. H. KEMPE, EDS., *Child Abuse and Neglect: The Family and the Community* (Cambridge, Ma., Ballinger, 1976). Recent effort to update the field in order to help individuals working in child abuse and neglect to implement effective, efficient and co-ordinated programmes of family assessment, treatment and learning both in the United States and abroad. Stress here is on assessing family interaction and pathology and family oriented therapy, and the community's response to the needs. There is an important section on early recognition and prevention of potential problems with family intervention.

C. H. KEMPE, R. E. HELFER, EDS., *Helping the Battered Child and his Family* (Philadelphia, Lippincott, 1974). A collection of contributions, primarily from members of the National Center for the Prevention and Treatment of Child Abuse and

Neglect in Denver focusing on treatment modalities available to individuals and communities using the concepts of lay health visitors, lay therapists or parent aides, crisis nurseries, individual and group therapy by a variety of professionals.

HAROLD MARTIN, ED., *The Abused Child: A Multidisciplinary Approach to Developmental Issues and Treatment* (Cambridge, Ballinger, 1976). A companion volume to *Child Abuse and Neglect: The Family and the Community*, it focuses for the first time exclusively on the child while the preceding volume focuses on the family. The contributers to this book are members of the National Center for the Prevention and Treatment of Child Abuse and Neglect in Denver, who have worked with abused and neglected children for many years who share their observations on diagnosis and individual and group treatment of children and the long term effects of child abuse on child development.

B. D. SCHMITT, ED., *The Child Protection Team Handbook* (New York, Garland, 1977). A concise presentation for community based or hospital based interdisciplinary child protection teams with a wealth of examples and standard forms which have evolved over the past years from the Denver group. The contributors are members of the Child Protection Team at University of Colorado Medical Center in Denver whose interdisciplinary team has now had twenty years of experience. Of special value are the appendices which present the problem oriented records for family evaluation and the development of treatment plans.

# Subject Index

# Index of Names

Another **Developing Child** title
edited by Jerome Bruner, Michael Cole
and Barbara Lloyd
from Fontana/Open Books

# Mothering
RUDOLPH SCHAFFER

As yesterday's children, today's parents. or tomorrow's parents-to-be, we all have direct experience of mothering. And yet its nature remains mysterious.

Is it an instinct, from which battering and neglect are rare and pathological deviations, or is it a skill which develops 'on the job'?

Recognizing the complexities of the relations between a mother and her child, Rudolph Schaffer is centrally concerned with the question of whether mothering is essentially a matter of physical care, or of attitude, or of stimulation; or whether, on the other hand, it is a reciprocal, synchronized activity in which the role of the infant, even of the new-born, is a far from passive one.

In *Mothering*, Rudolph Schaffer brings together the evidence, drawn from many recent studies and research projects, that can lead us not only to a clearer understanding of what is necessary for effective mothering, but to an assessment of the influence of the child's first attachment on his later emotional life, and of the significance or otherwise of the frequently cited 'blood bond' and 'mothering instinct'.